CASA SANTA FE

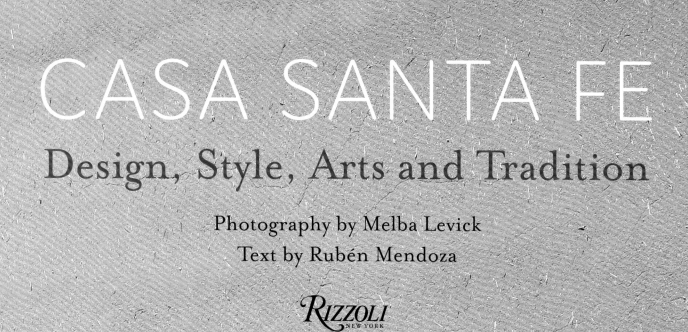

CASA SANTA FE

Design, Style, Arts and Tradition

Photography by Melba Levick

Text by Rubén Mendoza

RIZZOLI
NEW YORK

New York Paris London Milan

Dedicated to the late Arnold Joseph Wanya, Jr., and the indomitable Antonio Chavarria, Pueblo descendants of the communities of Acoma/Hopi, and Santa Clara, New Mexico.

And to the inspired architects, preservationists, and promoters of the Pueblo Revival styles of northern New Mexico, architects Isaac H. Rapp (1854–1933) and John Gaw Meem (1894–1983); archaeologists Edgar L. Hewitt, Jesse L. Nusbaum, and Sylvanus G. Morley; and the official photographer of the School of American Archaeology and the Museum of New Mexico, Carlos Vierra.

CONTENTS

INTRODUCTION

SOME YEARS AGO, I was honored to have been escorted into the heart of the twelfth-century Hopi village of Old Oraibi on Third Mesa by my Acoma Pueblo friend and fellow graduate student, the late Arnold Joseph Wanya Jr. Despite being raised in the equally ancient "Sky City" of Acoma in west central New Mexico, A. J. was deeply conflicted over his allegiance to his father's clan at Acoma, and that of his mother's at Old Oraibi. Arriving at *Orayvi* well after midnight, and without the benefit of a portable light source for penetrating the shroud of darkness that enveloped the ancient buildings and ruins all about us, A. J. summoned his grandmother from her sleep to request the key to the House of the Sun Chief. With the key in hand, I couldn't help but notice the affixed Bakelite plastic hotel tag reading *El Tovar*.

Wandering into the night, A. J. and I eventually approached a mud-covered masonry room block replete with a turquoise-blue screen door. We soon entered the ancient dust-laden dwelling located at the southeast end of the mesa. My first encounter with the ghostly specter of ruinous buildings fronting a moonlit dance plaza was the stuff of an otherworldly conjuring of the ancestors, and that through the veil of magical realism. At that moment, I spied the silhouette of a towering Spanish mission ruin standing at the edge of the mesa top. Upon entering the House of the Sun Chief, I was overcome with both a sense of wonderment and dread, for it was clear that I'd entered a restricted and most sacred ancient space. My reverence for the building was tempered by the knowledge that the Hopi, and the Pueblos more generally, saw in such spaces the embodiment of a living, breathing being or spirit to whom they offered maize pollen for its sustenance.

After lighting an antique miner's lantern, the space soon came alive with *katsina* earth and sky spirits, as well as masks, leggings, drums, rattles, flutes, and other ritual paraphernalia stacked high throughout the room. Having taken the cot by the window overlooking the darkened dance plaza, I lay back in awe of the reality that the entirety of the peeled-beam, or viga, ceiling was awash in an awesome array of eagle and colorful parrot feathers. At that moment, I abruptly exited the room and stood just outside of the ancient mud-covered limestone enclosure to pay my respects, and thereby recited aloud the Lord's Prayer in Nahuatl, the Uto-Aztecan language of the Mexica Aztec with whom I most identified at that time. My friend was perplexed

Opposite: Kiva ladder, Sky City, c. twelfth-century settlement, mid-seventeenth-century build. Acoma Pueblo, New Mexico.

by my actions, and I explained that I had felt I did not belong in that room, as it was a revered space of and for the ancestors, and an outsider like me had no place in that hallowed building. Upon reentering the enclosure, I returned to the cot, and as I looked back at the turquoise door, a large black spider entered and stood at the threshold. I called out to warn A. J. of our guest and A. J., who was already ensconced in a sleeping bag on the floor, told me to "kill the spider," to which I replied, "but what of Spider Woman?"

What happened that evening manifested in my dreams, and in those of A. J. and our travelling companion, Sharon Quickbear of the Rosebud Sioux Reservation. Though Sharon was taken in for accommodations on Second Mesa by the Bear Clan, that evening she too shared the ghostly apparition of the Spider Woman in her dream state, replete with shiny long black hair and ebony eyes. Each of us experienced an otherworldly visitation that left A. J. in fear of having offended the ancestors. Such was his concern that when, on the next day, during the katsina Bean Dance, his uncle handed him parrot feathers because "it is your time" to become a katsina, A. J. initially refused the sacred gift. He later begrudgingly accepted the parrot feathers, though he subsequently handed them to me for safekeeping. I too tried to convince him to accept them to honor his ancestors, but he insisted that I safeguard the parrot feathers for him should he relent. Though A. J. passed away not so long after that experience, I continue to hold his parrot feathers in trust as though awaiting the return of this grandson of the Sun Chief, and heir to a two-thousand-year-old tradition anchored to the *nan-sipu*, "belly-root" or "heart of the earth," and its precious children, the Ancestral Pueblo people and their descendants.

Santa Fe de San Francisco de Asís

The place we call Santa Fe was long known to the Tewa-speaking Pueblos of the region as Ogha Po'oge, or "White shell water place," and was rebranded and designated the province of Santa Fe de Nuevo México by the explorer and conquistador Juan de Oñate in 1610. Subsequently, the newly appointed governor of the province, Don Pedro de Peralta, christened the site of Santa Fe in the name of Saint Francis of Assisi, and such was La Villa Real de la Santa Fe de San Francisco de Asís founded. Santa Fe has a long and storied history, and an equally compelling architectural heritage antedating the arrival of the Spanish, Mexican, and American newcomers by nearly a thousand years. Situated at an elevation of 7,199 feet, or 2,194 meters, above sea level, Santa Fe is both the oldest and highest state capital in the United States. Its succession as the seat of power for a long line of Spanish, Mexican, and American governors and government officials has continued through virtually the entirety of its history. As such, Santa Fe, "The Royal Town of the Holy Faith of Saint Francis of Assisi," continues to elicit questions, and prompt historical revelations, which in turn continue to fuel speculation regarding the relative antiquity of the site and its settlement over the course of centuries. In fact, the construction of the Spanish colonial Palacio de los Gobernadores on the main plaza marked both the introduction of a standardized process for the production of Andalusian form-molded and sun-dried adobe brick technologies in the region, and thereby, the initial introduction for what we today most identify with the Santa Fe Style.

The Old Palace

Dated to circa 1610 and built under the authority of Governor Pedro de Peralta (1584–1666), the Palacio de los Gobernadores, or Palace of the Governors, was one of the first government buildings constructed anywhere in the region. As such, it housed a succession of Spanish governors dispatched from Mexico City and the Viceroyalty of New Spain through 1821, and thereafter Mexican provincial governors through 1848. Accordingly, the Pueblo Revolt of 1680 saw the Palace revert to the custody of the Pueblo leaders who drove the Spanish from New Mexico at that time, and it was they who occupied the Palace through to the *reconquista*, or reconquest, of the region by the Spanish, in 1693–94. During the occupation of the Palace of the Governors by the Pueblo people, they reintroduced puddled adobe or clay flooring and related Puebloan architectural preferences. From 1848 through 1892, American territorial governors and their staff occupied the building, and they too introduced architectural modifications such as New England and Greek Revival stylistic elements, including doors and window treatments identified with the territorial styles of the day.

In time, the building's deteriorating condition resulted in its abandonment, as the building was eventually deemed unsalvageable. Perhaps the best affirmation of the structure's condition as of 1906 is that offered by Governor Lew Wallace, and cited in the *National Trust Guide*, in which Wallace is quoted as contending that "The walls were grimy, the undressed boards of the floor rested flat upon the ground.... The cedar rafters, rain-stained as those in the dining-hall of Cedric the Saxon, and over-weighted by tons and tons of mud composing the roof, had the threatening downward curvature of a shipmate's cutlass." Deemed the oldest public building in the continental United States, the Old Palace was nevertheless threatened with demolition, and it was then that a coalition of area archaeological and historical societies prompted acquisition of the building by the Archaeological Institute of America. From that point forward, the Old Palace would serve a variety of purposes, including that of the home of the Museum of New Mexico, the School of American Archaeology, and accordingly, the headquarters of the New Mexico Historical Society. From this admixture of archaeologists, anthropologists, historians, and preservationists evolved the justly famous School of Advanced Research, whose campus plant is dominated by Spanish Pueblo and Mission Revival buildings of only the finest caliber.

Los Adobes

Puddled clay walls or mud floors with mud-covered flat-roofed timber vigas and *latilla* construction techniques are largely construed as forming the demarcation distinguishing Ancestral Pueblo or Anasazi from Spanish colonial building methods, but the reality is quite different. In truth, form-molded adobe bricks predate the Spanish entradas, or incursions, into the American Southwest by centuries, and have been recovered from securely dated Ancestral Pueblo or Anasazi archaeological contexts dating to AD 1250. The Ancestral Pueblo materials bore no evidence of fingerprints in their production, thereby implying the use of wooden or earthen forms; tempering or binding agents included ash, sand, gravel, and pottery fragments. By contrast, Spanish or Iberian-sourced adobes were generally fabricated from standardized wood-frame forms, with binding agents including straw, manure, and other material. The *Adobe Conservation Preservation Handbook* produced by the Santa Fe-based Cornerstones Community Partnerships, a 501(c)3 non-profit chartered in 1986 and devoted to adobe conservation in New Mexico and the US Southwest, has long acknowledged the nine-thousand-year-old pedigree and time depth of adobe origins in the Middle East, and its diffusion by way of Al-Andalus, or Andalusian Spain, the Middle East, and North Africa. Moreover, the antiquity of both puddled adobe wall construction and form- and hand-molded or paddle- and anvil-formed adobes spans the whole of the American hemisphere from the most remote times at such monumental sites as Moche, Peru (AD 100–700), to Comalcalco, Tabasco, Mexico (AD 600–1000), where inscribed and kiln-fired brick was all the rage.

Finally, before proceeding with our overview of the Ancestral Pueblo origins and affinities identified with the inspiration for the Santa Fe Style and its timeless adobes, it should be noted that the very term *adobe* per se is thought to draw from the Egyptian hieroglyph for *tob*, which in turn may have given rise to the Arabic term *ottob* or *al-Tub*, and by extension, via Andalusia, *adobe*. Having established the centrality of adobe, puddled adobe architecture, and its role in the Santa Fe Style, we now turn to a review of the two pivotal ancestral building traditions that gave rise to the Santa Fe Style, and by extension, the Pueblo, Spanish, Spanish Pueblo, Mission, and Territorial Revival movements.

The Ancestral Pueblo

The majestic landscapes of the high deserts of northern New Mexico have long proven a lure to those in search of a promised land. With the waters of the indomitable Rio Grande to the west and the Sangre de Cristo Mountains to the east, the place today identified with the town and region of Santa Fe was long ago called up by the ancestors as but one of a host of prophetic destinations or gathering places situated along the length and breadth of the snake-like course of the Rio Grande, the Guardian of the Waters, or Awanyu of the Pueblos. Ancestral Pueblo emigres processing from parched and distant ancestral homelands of the north and west gradually saw the fissioning of their ancient and profoundly sacred clans in a contest for survival, and, thereby, the cultural survivance of a seventeen-hundred-year-old way of life. Long before the thirteenth-century Puebloan diaspora that bore witness to the uprooting of ancestral villages and monumental masonry pueblos such as those of Chaco Canyon, New Mexico, Mesa Verde, Colorado, and Canyon de Chelly, Arizona, the tenor and quality of life, art, and the architectural traditions of that time were literally set in stone. With over one hundred monumental masonry Chacoan towns and Pueblo villages interconnected by a vast and particularly sophisticated road network spanning hundreds of miles, the Chacoan world's reach spanned much of the US Southwest. As such, trade, exchange, communication, social networks, and clan migrations were secured through the reach of time. At Chaco Canyon, the Ancestral Pueblo constructed the monumental eight-hundred-room "Great House" of Pueblo Bonito between the years of AD 828–1126. Its construction, which required the quarrying of fifty thousand tons of sandstone and the felling of some fifty thousand ponderosa pine (*Pinus* sp.), Douglas fir (*Abies* sp.), and Engelmann spruce (*Picea* sp.) trees located in intermontane groves thirty-eight to fifty miles distant, resulted in the creation of one of the earliest and largest buildings of its time anywhere in North America. The monumental Great Kivas of this time were clearly

central places at which Ancestral Pueblo clans from across the vast expanse of the Pueblo world convened. Recent studies of Chaco, Mesa Verde, Aztec, Betatakin, and a host of other Ancestral Pueblo or Anasazi sites by legions of archaeologists and scientists have made clear the complexity and sophistication of Chacoan civilization. The architectural heritage of the Ancestral Pueblo has similarly been construed as among the most sophisticated in the American hemisphere in terms of urban planning, building design and technology, and agricultural and hydraulic systems, and these long antedating the arrival of the first in a succession of Spanish explorers and conquistadores, and by the nineteenth century, Mexican and American interlopers, invaders, and settlers.

Top: Pueblo Bonito, c. AD 850–1250, Chaco Culture National Historical Park, New Mexico.

Bottom: Crib logged roof of Great Kiva, c. twelvth to thirteenth centuries, Aztec Ruins National Monument, New Mexico.

The Rio Grande Pueblos

Prompted by the vagaries of climate change, overpopulation, deforestation, habitat destruction, and drought, the Great Towns of the Ancestral Pueblo collapsed and were abandoned in unison. The catastrophic consequences of the Great Drought of AD 1130 through 1180 prompted region-wide Puebloan abandonments in the American Southwest throughout the twelfth and thirteenth centuries. Moreover, violent conflict and raiding activity by invaders and the influx of newcomers from the Mogollon Mountains, High Plains, and Great Basin exacerbated the already tenuous foothold of the Pueblos in their ancestral homelands. The influx of Athabaskan-speaking Diné or Navajo, Comanche, and Apache ultimately transformed the cultural and historical landscape of the Pueblo world for all time. In the wake of this historic reckoning with Mother Earth, the People conjured the ancestors by way of song, dance, prayers, and pilgrimage, and in so doing, gave birth to the katsina, whose emergence from the parched earth and sacred kivas, or earthen and masonry ceremonial pithouse structures and clan lodges, of the ancestors signaled new beginnings and first foundings. Consequently, some seven centuries ago the birth and/or return of the katsinas prompted the apparition of clan totems, otherworldly warriors, and water guardians across the expanse of the high desert and its sacred landscapes. Soon, the land was populated with rock art surrogates and supernaturals in the form of pecked rock petroglyphs and painted red ochre pictographs depicting revered ancestors, ancestral clans, *Kokopelli* water conjurers, and katsina spirits, whose variegated otherworldly powers marked the earth and the pathways of the ancestors and gave life to the magical world and rebirth of the Pueblo people.

In time, the displacement of the Ancestral Pueblo of the Four Corners gave birth to the legendary Pueblos of the Rio Grande Valley. The sheer magnitude of the region-wide abandonments that largely depopulated thirteenth-century northwestern New Mexico, northeastern Arizona, southeastern Utah, and southwestern Colorado ushered in the ruination of the century's old architectural wonders of the ancient world of the Ancestral Pueblo. In time, the renascent Pueblo peoples were reborn from the lifeblood of the Rio Grande with its fertile margins, such that scores of newfound Pueblo settlements flourished in these new lands from the thirteenth century onward. In the wake of this cataclysmic transformation of the cultural landscapes of the Four Corners, the sacred river that was the Rio Grande became home to the Puebloan peoples and their puddled adobe and mud-coated multistoried and/or subterranean masonry buildings or pueblos, kivas, plazas, and towers. Soon the bottomlands of the Rio Grande valley became the site of a wondrous new social experiment, with its panoply of architectural forms and curvilinear lines, canal-based irrigation systems, monumental multistoried apartment dwellings, turquoise mining and craftsmanship, and an extensive system of trade and exchange spanning the whole of the region, extending from the modern towns and cities of Las Vegas, New Mexico, to Las Vegas, Nevada, and from Durango, Colorado, to Durango, Mexico.

Cliff Palace,
c. AD 1150–1300.
Mesa Verde National
Park, Colorado.

Through the course of the next two centuries, the Pueblos that formerly occupied sites as far afield as Mesa Verde, Colorado; Chaco Canyon, New Mexico; and the Hopi Pueblos of northeastern Arizona converged en masse or in part on the Rio Grande and its tributaries. The newfound villages and pueblos of this diasporic people were founded anew at Acoma Pueblo, Cochiti, Hopi, Isleta, Jemez, Kewa, Laguna, Nambé, Ohkay Owingeh, Picuris, Pojoaque, San Felipe, San Ildefonso, Sandia, Santa Ana, Santa Clara, Santo Domingo, Taos, Tesuque, Zia, and Zuni. Each of these pueblos have weathered the vagaries of the high desert, with its snow-capped mountains on the one hand, and arid landscapes on the other, all the while maintaining traditional and sacred lifeways borne of thousand-year-old ancestral visions, customs, beliefs, and practices.

Such was the tenacity of the Puebloan people that they pioneered the development of dry farming, waffle gardens, shell and turquoise mosaics, pendants and amulets, a variety of musical instruments, food-processing technologies, polychrome murals, an elaborate symbol system and ritual iconography, extensive road and canal systems, and multistoried puddled-mud and masonry structures, including aboveground masonry granaries for storing the abundance borne of the "Three Sisters" whose earthly incarnation saw the growth and appearance of maize, beans, and squash. Drawing on this triad of fundamental staples, the Pueblos expanded upon these offerings with an extensive culinary menu, replete with domesticated

Betatakin cliff dwellings, c. AD 1250–1300. Navajo National Monument, Arizona.

turkey, and a variety of chiles, melons, nopal cacti, sunflower seeds, nuts, berries, deer, rabbit, and other small game.

Trade and exchange with peoples to the south and west spawned a network of social, cultural, ideological, and economic interactions with the peoples of western Mexico, the Sea of Cortez, and southern California, who all provisioned access to cacao, parrot feathers, copper repoussé, and marine shell used in the production of prestige goods and ritual paraphernalia deployed in katsina and kiva contexts across the Greater Southwest. Many of the trails and waterways that defined the course of centuries of long-distance interactions both within and beyond the high deserts of northern New Mexico eventually saw the arrival of Iberian and Mexican Indian colonists and settlers who introduced their own respective cultures, beliefs, technologies, building traditions, and languages.

The Spanish

First contact by the Ancestral Pueblo with Europeans, or more specifically, an enslaved North African Berber born Mustafa Zemmouri of Azemour, Morocco, came to pass in 1535. Initial contact was ultimately made by Mustafa, whose adopted Portuguese name was Esteban de Dorantes, with the people of Hawikuh, a Zuni pueblo, in 1539. Esteban was one of four survivors of the ill-fated *La Florida* expedition under the command of explorer and conquistador Pánfilo de Narváez, whose expeditionary force of some six hundred soldiers and forty-two horses was reduced to eighty starved and desperate shipwrecked survivors left to eating their horses after finding themselves off what is now the Texas coast in 1528. Soon thereafter, many of the crew perished, and Esteban, Cabeza de Vaca, Castillo, and, ironically, his Portuguese master Andreas Dorantes, were enslaved for some six years by indigenous communities hostile to the arrival of the interlopers. Upon their escape in 1534, the four survivors trekked across much of the region identified with the Gulf lowlands and US Southwest in an effort to return to Panuco, Mexico, to rendezvous with the Spanish settlements in that region. During these eight years, six spent in captivity, Esteban developed fluency in six native languages, and his Black skin proved his salvation, as the native communities that he interacted with believed him a powerful figure or medicine man. Upon returning to Mexico City, Dorantes sold Esteban to Viceroy Antonio de Mendoza in 1536. This fateful encounter would soon provoke a clash of cultures, which produced an iconic bifurcation of traditions, spanning language and culture, social interaction, ritual and religion, cosmology and belief, political ecologies and ideologies centered on the stewardship and ownership of the land, and ultimately, the proliferation of folk art, material culture, and architecture.

Cycles of Conquest

While at this juncture it would be apropos to acknowledge and review the exploits, explorations, and conflicts that arose when a succession of Spanish explorers, conquistadores, and soldiers of fortune entered the enchanted landscapes of New Mexico and the Greater Southwest, the complexity of such interactions is well beyond the scope of our studied consideration of the Santa Fe Style. Suffice it to say that the expeditionary force of 1540–42, dispatched by Viceroy Antonio de Mendoza and commanded by Francisco Vasquez de Coronado in search of the fabled Seven Cities of Gold or Cíbola, was fraught with conflict, death, and hardship. With some two thousand Sonoran Indian, Nahua, and Purepecha Indian allies guarding his flank and serving as scouts and translators, Coronado's Mexican Indian allies aided and abetted contact with the Pueblos, and their support proved formidable. Accordingly, the dire consequences of the expedition's goals, aligned with the challenges of the impending winter snows and food shortages, prompted a war of *sangre y fuego*, or blood and fire, that further intensified Pueblo resistance and prompted the resettlement of whole pueblos to defensive mesa-top locations. Though this same expedition charted the course from Mexico City and the Viceroyalty of New Spain to the heart of the Ancestral Pueblo homeland, a legacy of historical trauma would follow. Ancillary expeditions that spun off of the main expeditionary force ultimately "discovered" the Colorado River and Grand Canyon, explored the length and breadth of the Rio Grande with its many ancient pueblos, and trekked as far afield as what are known today as Kansas, the Texas Panhandle, and the Great Plains. Even so, the tragic consequences of the encounter visited upon the Pueblo people of such sites as Hawikuh, Acoma, Pecos, and the Pueblos of the Southern Tiwa of the Tiguex Province by the soldiers of the Coronado expedition formed the basis of what would haunt the Spanish colonial entradas by soldiers, missionaries, and colonists for centuries to come.

After a litany of brutal encounters between the Spanish and the Pueblo, as both perpetrators and defenders, the predictable retaliatory strikes by each party extended the scope of conflict through much of the next century. The memory of such encounters with a succession of Spanish conquistadores, and the systematic and sustained efforts by Franciscan missionaries to extinguish Pueblo religion and ritual, ultimately culminated in the Pueblo Revolt of 1680. The overwhelmingly decisive, and strategically coordinated, pan-Pueblo uprising was fomented under the leadership of Popé, or Po'pay, from Ohkay Owingeh, or San Juan Pueblo. The revolt, launched on August 10, 1680, spanned eleven days, and sought the wholesale expulsion of the Spanish colonists. Centered as it was on the province and town of Santa Fe de Nuevo México, the community of Santa Fe and its Palace of the Governors would ultimately prove ground zero, resulting in the deaths of some four hundred Spanish and Mexican Indian allies and twenty-two of thirty-seven Franciscan missionaries, and the expulsion of over two thousand colonists. As a millenarian movement inspired by the brutal suppression of Pueblo belief and tradition, Po'pay demanded the destruction and suppression of all things Spanish. The resulting conflagration saw the burning of Franciscan mission churches spanning the whole of the region, extending from the Rio Grande through to the Hopi Mesas and Old Oraibi, Acoma, and some of the largest pueblos on record, such as that at Pecos. Twelve years later, the Spanish launched the reconquista of the region, and the Rio Grande and its pueblos were secured for the Viceroyalty of New Spain and the colonial venture and transformations that would follow. Ironically, as Apache, Ute, and Comanche raids took a toll on both Pueblo towns and Spanish villas, the colonists soon realized that the pueblos were far more defensible than their own villas and walled and fortified *parajes*,

Top: El Santuario de Chimayo, c. AD 1816. Chimayo, New Mexico.

Bottom: San Francisco de Asís Mission Church, c. AD 1772–1816. Rancho de Taos, New Mexico.

or roadside inns. The latter, though spaced a day's ride apart and intended as way stations and campsites for the colonial caravans from Mexico City, predominated along the entire length of the almost 1,600-mile-long El Camino Real de Tierra Adentro connecting Santa Fe to Mexico City. Among the more notable such *parajes* that have survived are those of the Rancho de las Golondrinas, situated fifteen miles southwest of Santa Fe; La Hacienda de los Martínez, located seventy miles to the north-northeast and just south of Taos Pueblo; and the Plaza del Cerro in Chimayo, or Zimayo, twenty-eight miles north of Santa Fe.

Arquitectura Española

Mardith Schuetz-Miller, one of the foremost architectural historians of the Spanish and Mexican eras in the American Southwest, has produced a voluminous database or Biofile centered on the builders and buildings of early Hispanic California and the Southwest. In so doing, Schuetz-Miller has catalogued the names of a particularly diverse cadre of Spanish colonial and Mexican architects, stonemasons, carpenters, sculptors, metal workers, and other tradesmen and women documented to have had a hand in the construction of many of the Spanish missions, Mexican churches, chapels, friaries, and government buildings that once graced settlements as far afield as San Antonio, Texas, and Monterey, California. Though the approximately five hundred founding colonists of Santa Fe were registered in the census undertaken by the military of the early seventeenth century, only a quarter of these were identified as *gente de razón*, or "people of reason," and these were listed by name. The balance of the cohort of Spanish settlers, therefore, were likely of mixed race, *mestizo*, and predominantly Mexican Indians, documented to have consisted largely of Tlaxcaltecan and Sonoran Indian allies, who were permitted to found their own settlements as a concession for their loyalty and servitude to the crown. With this particularly diverse ensemble of colonists, Mexican Indian architectural traditions were introduced side by side with those deemed Spanish and Andalusian.

Top: Pueblo de Taos, c. AD 1000–1450. Taos Pueblo, New Mexico.

Bottom: Rancho de las Golondrinas, c. early eighteenth century. Santa Fe, New Mexico.

The Spanish Royal Corps of Engineers

Among those revelations credited to architectural historians, architects, and archaeologists specializing in the building trades and traditions of the Viceroyalty of New Spain or Mexico are those centered on the role of the Spanish Royal Corps of Engineers, whose contributions have often gone largely unheralded in the histories of civic, ceremonial, military, religious, and hydraulic engineering in North America. Established in 1711, under the eighteenth-century Bourbon Reforms, the Corps was tasked with addressing the defense of the Spanish borderlands. Among those introductions credited to the Spanish Royal Corps of Engineers are those specific to the building of public works and defensive systems, spanning Mission churches, town planning, public buildings, presidio forts and fortifications, defensive walls and features, and masonry aqueducts, mills, fountains, baths, and canals. A host of other water works, such as that of the massive and complex Acequia Madre irrigation ditch of the Los Angeles Basin of Alta California, and by extension, the construction and improvement of a host of water works such as that of the seventeenth-century Acequia Madre that parallels the street of the same name on Santa Fe's historic east side. Drawing on engineering principles developed over the course of centuries based on both Greco-Roman and Arabic antecedents, and indigenous architectural traditions in both Spain and from throughout the Americas, Santa Fe's architectural heritage was borne of a fusion of Amerindian, Greco-Roman or Vitruvian, Andalusian Mudéjar, and North African or Berber traditions and building practices.

The Ten Books of Architecture

Where adobe and masonry construction are concerned, the seat of the Spanish Viceroyalty of New Spain based in Mexico City issued a litany of architectural standards for addressing construction in seismically active areas, and across the breadth of differing environmental zones with distinct resources and access issues. Mardith Schuetz-Miller's translation of an eighteenth-century journeyman's manual for architectural practice in Mexico City has proven a veritable revelation of tools, technologies, design, and engineering principles and practices that once dominated the standards that would make their way into the far-flung northern frontiers of the Viceroyalty of New Spain, and by extension, the province of Santa Fe de Nuevo México. In addition to a mastery of essential engineering principles, often predicated on the *Ten Books of Architecture* or *De architectura*, a first-century BC treatise on architectural theory by the Roman architect and military engineer Marcus Vitruvius Pollio, the engineers and architects of the Spanish Royal Corps of Engineers were responsible for elaborating design principles that permitted the installation of major public works from across the Viceroyalty of New Spain and the so-called Provincias Internas of the north Mexican frontier or Greater Southwest. As such, whether seen or unseen, the architectural standards of Mexico City, such as construction ratios of 1:3 or 1:5 to determine foundation depth to wall height, were elaborated across the frontier, and are represented in virtually every surviving Spanish colonial and Mexican adobe and masonry structure of New Mexico.

Santa Fe Style and Design

Among the most distinctive and most emulated features of Spanish colonial and Mexican-era adobes and masonry buildings identified with the five historic districts of Santa Fe, and the Santa Fe Style in particular, are those iconic dimensions of architecture; building materials; earth tones; blue, brown, or white wood door and window trim; and layout, landscape design, and the arts more generally. In addition to the use of adobe clays mixed with binders such as straw, sand, and ash, the predominant seventeenth-century building material was timber, used for adzed vigas and other wooden architectural elements. Piñon (*Pinus edulis*) and ponderosa pine (*Pinus ponderosa*) were both popular; today, ponderosa pine is most commonly used for adobe construction, although there is also a preference for Engelmann spruce (*Picea engelmannii*), thanks to its character and "lack of cracking." The early eighteenth-century *morada*, or meeting house, of the Penitente Brotherhood of the Pueblo de Abiquiú features many of the elements enumerated here. The morada was the sub-

Spanish hornos, also known as: behive ovens. Rancho de las Golondrinas, c. nineteenth century. Santa Fe, New Mexico.

ject of paintings by the famed artist and Abiquiú resident Georgia O'Keeffe, who immortalized this justly famous historic meeting house.

Encompassing eighteen percent of Santa Fe's urban area, the historic adobes, *jacales,* or pole and mud structures, and masonry buildings of the five historic districts feature such character defining features as (a) walled compounds, (b) elaborately carved *labor de menado* or Mudéjar-style wooden *puertas* or doors, or hand-adzed and pintled doors with shuttered *ventanas* or windows, gates, and gateways, (c) wrought iron *rejas* or window grills, (d) *ladrillo* or brick-like tiles, *azulejo* or sandstone pavers, or Talavera-tiled patios, (e) Andalusian-inspired *empedrado,* or pebble and cobble pavements replete with geometric patterns, (f) *jardines,* or lush Mediterranean-like gardens, (g) *portales* or wood and masonry arcades or galleries, (h) verandas, or roofed and open-air galleries or porches, (i) the *zaguán,* from the Arabic *istawán* or *uṣṭuwān,* used to refer to the central passageway or gateway corridor into the patio or vestibule of an adobe house and/or compound, (j) "beehive" *hornos* or open-air ovens, introduced to the Iberian Peninsula by the Moors, and by extension, to the Pueblos of New Mexico and the Greater Southwest, (k) *bancos,* or adobe and fixed wooden benches, and l) the so-called wood-burning indoor "kiva fireplace," with its beehive-like conical configuration, the product of the work of Pueblo and Hispanic women known as *enjarradoras* or plasterers, who built and perpetuated this introduced Iberian and Andalusian tradition. (As to the term "kiva fireplace," which originated

Penitente Morada de Abiquiú, c. AD 1730s. Pueblo de Abiquiú, New Mexico.

with the early twentieth-century Pueblo Revival movement of Santa Fe, Taos resident Anita Rodriguez makes clear that she and fellow Pueblo and Hispanic peoples deem the term politically and culturally insensitive.)

To this constellation of building details and design are to be added the typical *terrado* or *azotea*, flat earthen roofs assembled from hand-adzed vigas of ponderosa pine and other suitable timber. Often replete with *latillas* or peeled slats or sticks used to span vigas, the thick clay layers of adobe deployed as roofing material, or a *torta*, served to seal the roof and at the same time insulate rooms from the elements. Wooden corbels were characteristic of mission church architecture, but were also deployed in residential contexts, and while often ornately carved, essentially served as supports for vigas and rafters, whereas *zapatos* or wooden "shoes" were used as structural supports required to cap posts used to build *portales* or galleries and verandas. To this array of features were added hand-adzed wooden lintels and clay, ceramic, or wooden *canales* or roof drains projecting from the roof line of many a Santa Fe adobe. Finally, *nichos* or wall niches were inset at strategic points along the adobe walls both on the interior of homes and along the walls fronting the courtyard or patios of the day. The adjoining *cocinas* or kitchens, with their ceramic griddles or *comales*, for the production of tortillas and other food preparation, lent to the colorful panoply of *cerámicas* or hand-painted and glazed majolicas, azulejo and Talavera tile-work, and other Hispanic and Mexican-sourced and Pueblo pottery.

Origins of the Pueblo Revival

As an archaeologist and longtime historic preservationist with an expertise in the Spanish and Mission Revival architectural styles of California and the US Southwest, I take my lead from the *National Trust Guide* for Santa Fe by Richard Harris. As a former resident of Santa Fe, Harris returned to his hometown to write a guide to the adobes and other buildings in this historic town. Working through a host of challenges in the mid-1990s, Harris soon discovered that he faced the daunting task of identifying, selecting, and writing about a handful of the approximately ten thousand historically significant buildings recorded by the New Mexico Historic Preservation Department in Santa Fe. As a resident, Harris recalled the "disorienting" character of the so-called Santa Fe Style, the subject of this book. Largely bereft of the usual visual cues that define and distinguish the buildings of most American towns and cities, the absence of these proved disconcerting, and at the same time, unique to a town where virtually all buildings bore the appearance of the ancient Ancestral Pueblo or Anasazi, and Spanish or Mexican sunbaked adobe or puddled earthen building traditions of the period spanning the late thirteenth through mid-nineteenth centuries in the American Southwest. Unlike other such studies, Harris began his overview with the origins of the historic preservation movement as seen through the eyes of the early twentieth-century archaeologists and architects of Santa Fe.

Archaeology and the Santa Fe Style

The critical role played by Southwestern archaeologists in the development of the Santa Fe Style, or more specifically, its antecedents in the Spanish Pueblo Revival, has long been overshadowed by the monumental creations of those architects who followed in the footsteps of the original practitioners. In fact, noted Southwestern archaeologist Edgar Lee Hewett (1865–1946) proved pivotal in launching legislation that led to the passage of the Antiquities Act of 1906, which has served as the basis for virtually all such legislation bearing on the achievements of the historic preservation movement, and ultimately, the launch of the National Historic Preservation Act of 1966. The latter act served as the charter for the launch of the National Park Service's National Register of Historic Places, which accounts for some 1.8 million historic resources, including "buildings, sites, districts, structures, and objects," as of this writing.

Formative developments central to both the Antiquities Act and the National Historic Preservation Act began with Hewett's efforts to protect both the Pajarito Plateau, where Adolph Bandelier was engaged in archaeological investigations, and Chaco Canyon, which was under threat from looters. Hewett's alliance with Iowa congressman John F. Lacey, who had observed the looting and destruction of the region's archaeological resources first-hand, ultimately assured passage of the Antiquities Act of 1906. Shortly thereafter, and in his newfound capacity as founding director of the new School of American Archaeology, Hewett recruited archaeologist Jesse L. Nusbaum to undertake the "restoration" of the Spanish colonial Palace of the Governors on the Santa Fe Plaza, work that spanned the period from 1909 through 1913. It was here that the school was provisionally housed. Soon, Nusbaum in turn recruited longtime associate Sylvanus Griswold Morley for the task of the restoration, and the two revolutionized the idea of archaeological restoration. Those principles and practices launched within the context of the rehabilitation of the Old Palace would then be applied to the restoration of Mesa Verde, Colorado, and under the auspices of Morley, the Yucatecan Maya site of Chichen Itza. Moreover, Morley went on to purchase the Roque Lobato House of 1785, a home built by Spanish soldier Roque Lobato on a land grant deeded to him by then-Governor Juan Bautista de Anza for meritorious service to the Spanish crown in the Comanche Indian Wars. Morley's acquisition of the Roque Lobato House in 1910 provided the young Mayanist a platform for bolstering the historic preservation efforts of the School of American Archaeology. Ultimately, Morley sought to stave off the city's denigrating characterization as "archaic" and less than American at a time when New Mexico was being considered for statehood, which was granted in 1912, the very year that both he and Hewett were appointed to the Santa Fe City Planning Board. In that role, Morley launched an exhibition at the Palace of the Governors devoted to chronicling the "New-Old Santa Fe" and its architecture. According to Chris Wilson and Oliver Horn, Morley "suggested that they formulate a revival style based on the city's old architecture so that rather than a 'City Beautiful' Santa Fe would instead be the 'City Different.'" From that point forward, the quest to preserve and promote the historic adobes of Santa Fe moved forward expeditiously, and the imprint of the "City Different" would sway the pendulum from demolition and destruction to revival and emulation of the Pueblo, Spanish, and Territorial Revival styles that have since defined the character of Santa Fe.

The Architects

Like many of those inspired by the momentous restoration efforts undertaken by Southwestern archaeologists Edgar Lee Hewett and Jesse L. Nusbaum on the Santa Fe Plaza between 1909 and 1913, architect Isaac Hamilton Rapp (1854-1933) elaborated upon Hewett and Nusbaum's promotion of a fledgling Spanish Pueblo Revival Style for Santa Fe. The efforts by the School of American Archaeology team at the Palace of the Governors soon generated community interest in revitalizing the Plaza, and by extension, promoting a Spanish Pueblo Revival by area architects, planners, and city leaders. Rapp's contributions were such that he was soon identified as the originator of the style, in large part due to the buildings he designed and built between 1917 and 1920. Among these, the most notable include the New Mexico Museum of Fine Arts (1917), La Fonda (1922), the Santa Fe School for the Deaf (1916), and the Sunmount Sanatorium (1914, 1920).

Drawing on Rapp's noteworthy influence on the architectural trends initially introduced by the restoration of the Palace of the Governors, John Gaw Meem (1894-1983) is perhaps best known for what is today deemed the Santa Fe Style, as it was his contributions to the adobe landscapes and skyline of the "City Different" that were cemented into Santa Fe's building codes, and which became law in 1957. Inspired by Rapp's Spanish Pueblo Revivals, Meem's early works were centered on Canyon Road and the Acequia Madre historic district. He is best identified with the development of what has since come to be known as the Territorial Revival Style, most cogently expressed in the Americanized early adobe architecture of El Zaguán and the Borrego House on Canyon Road. The American Territorial Style, and the later nineteenth-century Railroad Style, were stylistically influenced by the opening of free trade to Santa Fe de Nuevo México by the newly formed Mexican government of 1821. With the ending of Spanish trade restrictions, Mexican trade and exchange with the US boomed along the length and breadth of the one-thousand-mile Santa Fe Trail. Extending from Franklin, Missouri, on the Missouri River to Santa Fe, New Mexico, the trail made way for the introduction of American building products, including appreciable quantities of window glass, milled lumber, and kiln-fired brick. When, in the 1880s, the Santa Fe Trail was displaced by the coming of the railroad, many of the extant adobes of Santa Fe were retrofitted to accommodate the American penchant for the Greek Revival Styles that once predominated in the eastern US in the period from 1820 through 1850. The Territorial Revival Style that redefined the architectural landscape of Santa Fe to the extent that it had was characterized by the use of kiln-fired brick-coping atop adobe walls, window glass, and gabled roofs made possible by the ready availability of milled lumber. It was the "revival" of this tradition in adobe renovations and new builds for which John Gaw Meem has been celebrated.

Since the earliest suite of contributions by Rapp and Meem, a stream of prominent and consequential architects, architectural historians, historic preservationists, planners, community activists, artists, photographers, and designers from all walks of life have galvanized their resolve to protect and preserve the historicity and heritage of the "City Different" in the "Land of Enchantment."

About this Book

When an internationally acclaimed architecture and design photographer and an archaeologist and architectural historian team up to produce a visually compelling overview of an ancient architectural tradition deeply steeped in both Amerindian and European architectural antecedents, the discovery process, challenges, and rewards can be many and legion. With Ancestral Pueblo, Spanish colonial, Mexican provincial, and early American Territorial traditions within our purview, the inherent richness of the cultural landscapes so noted far exceed anything that can be fully captured in a single visual and editorial endeavor. As we found with our first co-authored Rizzoli book, *The California Missions* (2018), each historic site and stylistic or modern spinoff possesses a multitude of possibilities, pitfalls, and potential challenges, not all of which can be addressed in a single treatment. Nevertheless, photographer Melba Levick and I, architectural historian Rubén G. Mendoza, accepted the challenge, and Rizzoli signed on to contract and support us in this formidable undertaking on February 27, 2020, on the eve of the onset of the Covid-19 pandemic. We began planning for both the scripting and scope of the undertaking, and Melba and I determined to do what she'd done on our second book, Rizzoli's *The Spanish Style House: From Enchanted Andalusia to the California Dream* (2021). In effect, to go native, so to speak, and launch a host of forays, both real and imagined, into the high deserts of northern New Mexico. Despite the constraints borne of the pandemic, we both scheduled exploratory ventures to Santa Fe to conduct site visits, shoot photographs, and meet, greet, and interview the owners, artisans, architects, and designers identified with the historic adobe, timber, and masonry homes being scouted for inclusion in this book. To launch this undertaking, I offered potential community contacts and longtime friends and associates available to introduce Melba to the shakers and movers deemed key to comprehending the histories and stylistic traditions of each home or building under consideration. Once introduced, Melba quickly began establishing contacts with people in the know, including gallery owners, realtors, and area architects and designers.

I in turn headed to Santa Fe on June 20, 2021, in order to embed myself in the community for a one-month stay at Tres Casitas, a delightful and wonderfully tranquil historic hundred-year-old adobe compound. I was lodged in one of the three *casitas*, in this case, La Casita Rosa, a viga-studded adobe, and Airbnb rental, on Santa Fe's east side. The proprietress, Tess (La Contessa, as she is called), proved a wonderful hostess, with a wealth of tales regarding the arts community and historic districts of Santa Fe, and memorable stories of her childhood in Madrid, Spain. Even the complimentary bottle of Grenache and the homemade apricot liqueur conjured stories of the history and personalities of Santa Fe. As soon became apparent, the adobe compound at Tres Casitas was ideally situated in a historic district within walking distance of the main plaza, and on an old dirt track named Calle la Paz. Located a stone's throw from the centuries-old Acequia Madre irrigation canal or "Mother Ditch" dated to circa 1680, the gurgling stream, like the courtyard fountain at Tres Casitas, lent to the tranquility of the place.

Adding to the historicity of the place, the *acequia* was originally sited along the east to west trending Ancestral Pueblo footpath lying between the Santa Fe River Valley and Pecos pueblo to the east. My adobe refuge ultimately proved ideal for an atmospheric and peaceful writing retreat, replete with its bright pink *milagro*-festooned gateway, wisteria-covered portal, tranquil three-tiered hand-hewn stone fountain, sandstone-covered patio, kiva fireplaces both within the adobe and nestled among the lush gardens boasting cherry and apricot trees, desert cacti, sage, and a host of perennials beautifully maintained by La Contessa. In the final analysis, we conceived *Casa Santa Fe: Design, Style, Arts and Tradition* as closure for the latest and third installment in a trilogy devoted to Amerindian and Hispanic architectural traditions and styles in California and the American Southwest. Like the architectural revivals and historic preservationists of the city of Santa Fe, this book too pays homage to the storied Pueblo and Hispanic peoples, and early American settlers of this "Land of Enchantment."

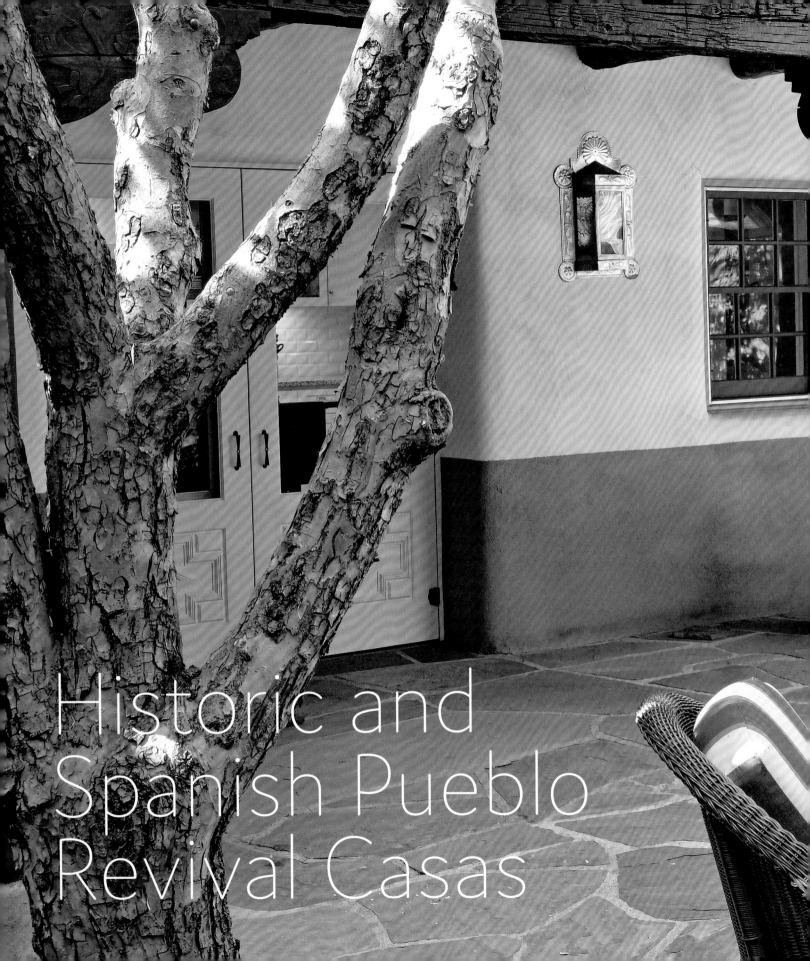

Historic and
Spanish Pueblo
Revival Casas

The Roque Lobato House
1785

The Roque Lobato House, or "House of the Spirits," was constructed by its namesake, a soldier and armorer of the Spanish garrison or presidio in 1785–86. Deemed one of Santa Fe's most significant historic homes by *The Magazine ANTIQUES* in 2007, the house underwent a thorough remodel by its current owners, Dr. Karl L. Horn and his wife, Susan, who engaged architect Craig Hoopes in the undertaking. The renovation was intended to evoke the era identified with famed Mayanist Sylvanus Griswold Morley, who purchased the house in 1910. Morley, known for his role as the director of the Carnegie expedition at Chichen Itza, and his espionage role as Agent 53 on behalf of the Office of Naval Intelligence during World War I, soon undertook renovations identified with the Spanish Pueblo Revival Style. The emerging historicist direction that Morley pursued nevertheless included the addition of board and batten wainscot, and the integration of a seventeenth- or eighteenth-century beam, post, and corbel arcade salvaged from a house on Arroyo Tenorio Street. Standout features of the house include eighteenth-century peeled-beam vigas, bancos, the aforementioned elaborately carved post and beam arcade, tin chandeliers and sconces crafted by Maurice Dixon, and a one-of-a-kind library designed and crafted by artisan Sergio Tapia. Moreover, the Horns embellished their home with the art and furnishings of Art Colony artisan William P. Henderson, whose Mission revival furnishings were a favorite of Sylvanus Morley, who relished their simplicity. Taken together, such features lend warmth and a cultured ambience to the home, and reflect its storied history, particularly that encompassing the years 1910 through 1930.

Tinwork, or *Hojalata*, consisting of ornamental, religious, and utilitarian items crafted in tin, has been dubbed the "poor man's silver." With sixteenth-century origins in New Spain or Mexico, many credit this craft to its beginnings in San Miguel de Allende. As with the crafting of silver, tin was pounded, punched, and stamped into a variety of works. Its early introduction into New Mexico experienced a resurgence when the Santa Fe Trail, and later, the US military introduced quantities of tin containers in the 1840s. Today, tinwork includes *nichos* or shadow boxes for saints and other religious objects, candelabras, mirror frames, crosses, sconces, ornaments, and jewelry. This spread includes tin chandeliers by Maurice Dixon in the Palla House and Robert Woodman at *Los Poblanos*, a ceiling lantern by Justin Gallegos Mayrant in the Hollenbeck House, and a nicho or shadow box by the Sandoval family in the Viera House.

Casa Donaciano Vigil
1832

Dating to the 1780s, this historic adobe was the home of Santa Fe city official Juan Cristóbal Vigil and his wife, María Antonia Andrea Martínez. Their son Donaciano inherited the property and its orchards in 1832, at which time he undertook renovations and the acquisition of adjacent properties. The son would go on to serve as a Mexican soldier and statesman, and second US territorial governor of New Mexico during the critical years of the Mexican American War and succeeding Mexican Cession of 1848. The adobe was the site of a host of major political actions and cultural activities spanning the transition into the Territorial era. The single-story adobe compound with a gated zaguán and an interior patio was the epicenter of a large estate fronting the Santa Fe River, and Donaciano continued to invest in real estate holdings as far afield as Pecos. In 1959, Chicago-born artist Charlotte White and her companion, sculptor Boris Gilbertson, thoughtfully refurbished the house. Drawing on salvaged historic doors and windows from the Loretto Academy, Charlotte and Boris saw through a remodeling that spanned 1972 through 1980. The current owner, Christopher Watson, again remodeled the house in 2017–19 in collaboration with designer Scott Cherry of Lightfoot Inc. Inspired by the work of Barcelona architect Gustau Gili, the latest remodel reflects Gili's sense of style. The house has since been added to the National Register of Historic Places, and the Historic Santa Fe Foundation in turn added the adobe to its Register of Resources Worthy of Preservation.

Casa Hankinson

1700s, 1930

Though its exact date of construction remains unknown, Casa Hankinson is thought to date to the 1700s, when it originally served as a Spanish mill. The building that once served as the mill was subsequently transformed into a single-family residence and was used as such through the 1990s. The ancient adobe admirably represents the Spanish Pueblo Revival Style and incorporates traditional Catalan-vaulted or *boveda* ceilings whose design origins in Spain date to the fourteenth century. Prior to purchasing the house in 2002, Donna and Hal Hankinson were longtime New Mexico residents, with twenty-seven years in the region. During those years they became quite familiar with historic adobe architecture, and upon seeing the old house knew that there was something truly special about it. The adobe exudes a distinctive old New Mexico charm, and an ambience that modern construction simply cannot replicate. From its old and beautiful Catalan-vaulted and beamed viga and latilla ceilings, *labor de menado* carved doors, elegantly carved corbels, kiva fireplaces, and a suite of interior woodwork designed and crafted by noted New Mexican architect William Lumpkins, the house speaks to its Spanish Pueblo Revival origins and influence. While there are no current project plans to further renovate or remodel, the Hankinsons remodeled the kitchen in 2009, the guest bath in 2019, built an outdoor pavilion, and its particularly lush grounds were landscaped by Alana Markel.

Casa Juan Rodriguez
1829

This adobe was originally built for the Juan Rodriguez family in 1829, and its design conforms to the Spanish Pueblo Style. Built on the site of an old Spanish grist mill dated to 1756, the Casa Juan Rodriguez was remodeled in 1960 by the famed New Mexico architect William Lumpkins. The remodeling of that time was extensive, with Lumpkins tasked with reviving the historic character of the old adobe. The building features original early nineteenth-century adobe walls and historic Mexican labor de menado and Spanish pueblo doors, as well as Catalan-vaulted or boveda ceilings and hand-hewn vigas. A small "crooked" window originally installed in 1844 is a character-defining feature deemed unique to the one-room adobes of the time. An eighteenth-century Spanish colonial altarpiece was integrated into the design of the elegant dining room of Casa Juan Rodriguez. The landscaping was the work of Joseph Bramlette. Previous owners include Mr. and Mrs. S. C. Hamilton, who acquired the property in 1923. The historic property was purchased by the current owners, Linda and Wayne Palla, in 2014.

Casa Carlos Vierra

1921

Casa Carlos Vierra was originally constructed by its namesake from 1918 through 1921. The Pueblo Revival Style adobe was designed, built, and owned by Carlos and Ada Vierra. Carlos Vierra was the first resident artist in Santa Fe, and proved his versatility as an archaeologist, architect, and photographer for the Palace of the Governors–based School of American Archaeology. Vierra constructed the 5,000-square-foot home within a compound on a two-acre parcel. The Vierras' home was not the only building on the grounds; the parcel included two casitas, as well as the only private indoor tennis court in Santa Fe. The tennis court, however, was built much later than the rest of the buildings on the site. According to the current owners, Joe and Bunny Colvin, the "home wraps its arms around you," and holds "so much history...If only the walls could talk." Their favorite feature is in fact Carlos Vierra's very own art studio, which includes a kiva fireplace that is among the most photographed in Santa Fe. Simply standing within its walls permits one to feel the history radiating from this historic adobe. The Colvins use the adobe as a second home, and they use the casa and compound to convene large events and fundraisers, and from time to time, some wonderful parties. In sum, the Casa Carlos Vierra is one of the most historically significant homes in Santa Fe.

KIVA FIREPLACES & HORNOS

The *fogón*, fireplace or fire box, that so typifies the Spanish Pueblo Revival Style of northern New Mexico was first introduced to the region by the Spanish in the sixteenth to seventeenth centuries. Consisting of a corner fireplace with an arched opening, the *fogón* was rebranded and popularized in the early twentieth century by Euroamerican builders and designers who came to call it the "kiva" fireplace. Though the name has endured, Ancestral Pueblo descendants question the use of the term *kiva,* which hearkens to the sacred ritual chambers and council houses of the Pueblo communities of the Four Corners region.

Unlike the *fogón* or "kiva" fireplaces that dominate the interiors of Santa Fe and northern New Mexico adobes, the *horno* has a decidedly different pedigree, form, and function. These outdoor beehive-shaped ovens with arched openings and smoke vents as opposed to chimneys serve almost exclusively as ovens for the baking of bread and the cooking or parching of other foodstuffs such as maize, and occasionally, the firing of pottery by the Pueblos. First introduced by the Spanish, these ovens have traditionally been constructed with adobe, or sun-dried mud bricks, and mud mortar and plaster, atop stone or adobe foundations. Their pedigree, however, began with the Muslims of north Africa who introduced these ancient ovens into the Iberian Peninsula in the twelfth century.

Meem Casas

Hollenback House
1932

Located on a hillside overlooking Santa Fe's historic east side, Hollenback House was designed and built by architect John Gaw Meem for New York heiress Amelia Hollenback in 1932. Meem saw this house as one of his most significant architectural achievements, while at the same time admitting that much of the credit must go to Hollenback. Deemed the best of Meem's Pueblo Revival homes, it features picturesque massing, peeled-beam vigas and latillas, kiva fireplaces, and vintage pueblo doors and windows salvaged from Gran Quivira, Acoma, Tesuque, and San Ildefonso and Spanish and Mexican villages, and Holleback proved instrumental in the design and curation of materials for the build. In fact, she prepared detailed lists of construction materials, including beam sizes and lengths, and numbers and sizes of vigas and latillas, which she acquired while residing near Tesuque Pueblo. Meem incorporated what Hollenback sent him, resulting in a beautiful, museum-quality collection of seventeenth- through nineteenth-century materials integrated into the house. Hollenback ultimately spent very little time living in the home and never returned to Santa Fe after 1947, leaving only her caretaker to tend to the home. Under the watchful eye of the new owners, Temple and Mickey Ashmore, the house underwent extensive remodeling from 2012 through 2020. Landscaping included a terraced garden replete with rose, lavender, native wildflowers, and other perennials, in addition to a vegetable garden, stone fire pit, and fountain. New doors were recently added to the service portal near the kitchen to create a true "solar portal" in the manner of John Gaw Meem.

Casa Salome Anthony
1924

Part of a three-structure compound designed and
built by John Gaw Meem in 1924, Casa Salome
Anthony was one of two adobe houses and a casita
built at that location. Meem originally constructed the compound for three women, Salome
Anthony, Maurice Meaders, and Bella Staples,
who lived in the historic compound for forty
years. Recent renovations to the home took place
in 2004–05, and these latest upgrades account
for the home's current appearance. The original
living room was remodeled into a library, and the
unique fireplace—one of four—is thought to have
been designed and built by Meem in collaboration
with William Penhallow Henderson. The current
owners, both retired architects, designed a new
portal as a part of a new freestanding building.
This recent addition contains an artist's studio
and guest quarters and is regularly used as a summer lodge by the current owners. Other distinctive features of the home include peeled-beam
vigas and latillas, blue-painted door-trim boards,
and coyote fencing. Donna Bone of Design with
Nature undertook the enhanced landscaping
specific to the east garden, with changes meant
to conjure a passive woodland ambience, replete
with aspen trees.

VIGAS, LATILLAS & CORBELS

Casa Hunt

1929

The original owner of this Pueblo Revival home, Fred Thompson, commissioned John Gaw Meem to build it in 1929. Thompson, an important figure in his own right, was the Santa Fe Garden Club president for several years. The main facade and portal evoke the style and design of Santa Fe's Palace of the Governors, which proved a pivotal inspiration to the Santa Fe Style from the outset. In addition, we may spy elements of the Territorial Revival Style as window treatments. Under the discerning eye of current owners Brad and Lauren Hunt, the home underwent a thorough remodel in 2015. Lauren designed the landscape, including a rectilinear stone wall using Southwestern masonry techniques typical of the early twentieth century. Native grasses provided a counterpoint to the stone and stucco hardscape. They are currently designing a studio for the back lot of the home. They have truly loved meshing the timeless Pueblo Revival house Meem designed and built with an updated modernist appearance.

Los Poblanos

1935, 2011

Los Poblanos is a wonderful farmhouse-style home in Los Ranchos de Albuquerque, New Mexico. The owners of the adjoining Los Poblanos Inn, Penny and Armin Rembe, constructed their Territorial Revival Style home to complement the ambience and style of the inn in 2011. On the sprawling Elena Gallegos land grant of 1716, the ranch was owned by Ambrosio and Juan Cristobal Armijo and their descendants through the nineteenth century. Subsequently, Albert and Ruth Simms acquired the 800-acre ranch in the 1930s and soon set about recruiting architect John Gaw Meem and a cadre of WPA artists and craftspeople to renovate the ranch house and transform the complex into their residence, and by extension, the La Quinta Cultural Center. Meem expanded the building with an L-shaped addition, added multiple white-painted portáles, and kept the older *fogónes* or corner fireplaces, and exposed vigas and corbels. With gardens designed by Rose Greely and design features by Meem, the grounds proved opulent. Once the epicenter for political and community events and recreation, the former cultural center and Los Poblanos Ranch headquarters have since been converted over to use as the Los Poblanos Inn, deemed "one of the most magnificent historic properties in the Southwest." Penny and Armin Rembe purchased the ranch in two phases between 1976 and 1999 and built their Territorial Revival home in 2011. As with the inn, bricked coping and white-painted portales are character-defining features, with the portales fronting a splendid patio courtyard replete with a beautifully tiled Mudéjar-style fountain.

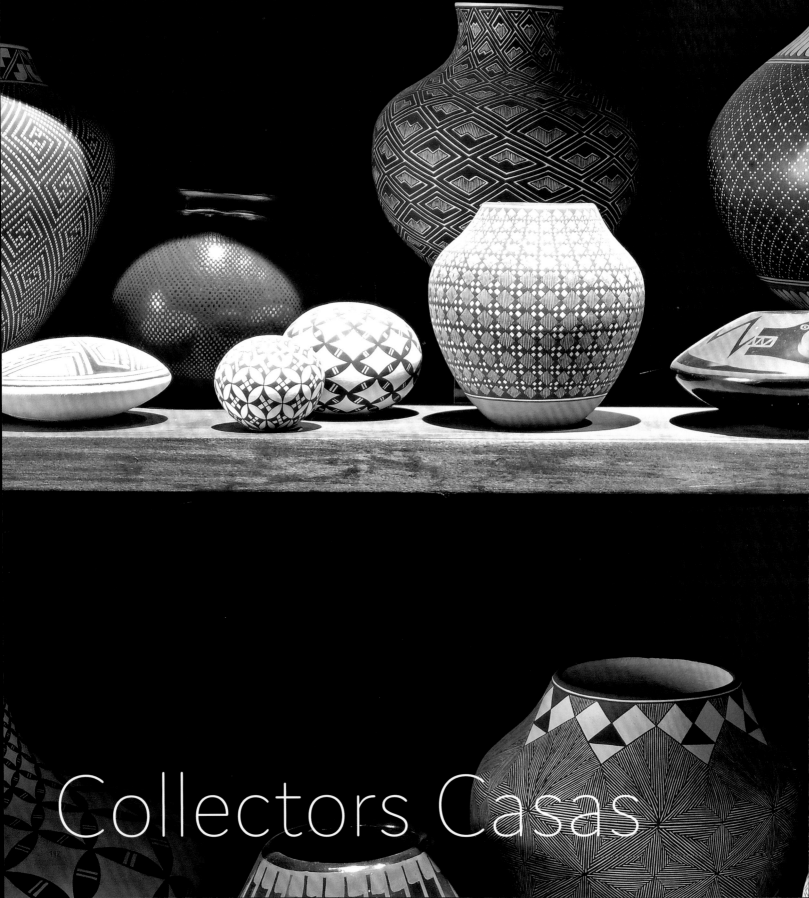

Collectors Casas

Ignacio de Roybal House

1350, 1705, 1932

When European explorers first entered the region today identified with Rancho Jacona or the Pueblo of Sakonae (Zha-kho-nai-i), the Spanish misinterpreted it as *Hah-ko-nah*, and it became Jacona thereafter. According to noted Southwestern archaeologist Adolph Bandelier, the people of Sakonae occupied the Pueblo from the mid-fourteenth through the late seventeenth centuries. Sakonae, lying on the Pojoaque River, was abandoned by the Pueblo people, along with other outlying hamlets, after the reconquista of Santa Fe by Diego de Vargas in 1692. They built the Ignacio Roybal House within the context of the original pueblo dating to circa 1350. Don Ignacio de Roybal y Torrado, the high sheriff for the Inquisition, acquired the property by purchase in 1705. The adobe remained in Ignacio de Roybal's family through 1932. Little changed from its formative beginnings, the house retains much of its historic fabric, including earthen floors, adobe walls, fogónes, vintage doors, beamed ceilings and latillas, and such later additions as the Territorial Revival window headers and framing. At one time, the main door featured the original lock from the old Pojoaque Church, which was destroyed by fire in the 1920s. Though contested by the Pueblo, the US government eventually granted the land patent to Porfirio Roybal in 1937, and later that year, acclaimed Western writer Jon Glidden, aka Peter Dawson, and his wife purchased the property. The Gliddens lovingly restored the property, which has since become the home of Andrea Fisher. Andrea has sought to preserve the original Spanish Pueblo Style of the home. The property was included in the Historic Santa Fe Foundation and the New Mexico State Register of Cultural Properties in 1976, and ultimately, the National Register of Historic Places, each of which acknowledged the site's historical significance.

CERAMICS

With an 1,800-year pedigree in the American Southwest, Pueblo pottery evolved from purely utilitarian wares and decorative ceremonial vessels through to the folk and fine art creations of today. Ancestral symbols that grace such vessels are those of the stepped-fret or cloud pattern, Awanyu water serpent, Kokopelli water conjurer, "Zia Bird" or roadrunner, the Zuni deer with heart line, Flower World imagery, and a vast array of geometric designs from such Pueblos as Santa Clara, Hopi, San Ildefonso, Acoma, Santo Domingo, and Zia. Prominent late nineteenth- and twentieth-century potters María and Julian Martinez of San Ildefonso and Nampeyo of Hano popularized the rebirth of these traditions.

The ancestral Pueblos of the Greater Southwest, including those of Arizona, New Mexico, Colorado, Utah, and northern Mexico, produced a spectacular array of earthenware pottery types spanning every conceivable use, form, and function. In effect, the pre-Contact era was awash in a pageantry of design, style, and art from the outset of this two-thousand-year-old tradition. Crafted from both alluvial and geological clays found throughout the region, clay slips used to coat the unfired vessels combined with iron oxides and micaceous clays and firing temperatures to produce a spectrum of color variations and types. Traditionally crafted by women, virtually all pre-Contact through recent examples are the product of the coiling and scraping, or paddle and anvil, methods that originated in remote antiquity. The Spanish introduction of the potter's wheel in the seventeenth century provided an alternative, but even so, the Pueblos maintain the ancestral methods, while Hispano descendants largely craft their wares atop the wheel. Firing techniques vary, but the earliest such methods drew on pit-kiln firing, whereas many of the Pueblos of the Rio Grande deploy above ground fires fed with juniper, mesquite, pine, and to a lesser degree cedar, or animal dung. Otherwise, Pueblo wares remain largely coil-built, stone or gourd polished, and wood or manure fired. The types and uses encompass cookware, serving dishes (including bean pots and stew bowls), ladles, cups, storage containers or *ollas*, seed jars, water bottles or canteens, wedding jars and effigy pots. The heritage vessels depicted here span nineteenth century Zuni Pueblo "deer with heart line" vessels, a nineteenth-century Zuni Pueblo bowl featuring the Morning Star motif, and eighteenth-century Zia Pueblo and nineteenth-century Zuni polychrome pottery canteens.

Juan José Prada House
1768, 1835

According to the Historic Santa Fe Foundation, early maps indicate that this adobe dates to circa 1768. It was first recorded as belonging to Juan José Prada, the son of José Prada, a Spanish soldier of the Santa Fe garrison, in 1869. Once divided into two buildings by a zaguán, the west half of the building was deeded to Altagracia Arrañaga, and the east half to Miguel Gorman, a descendant of one of the soldiers of the 1840s US Army occupation. In the late nineteenth century, a brick *pretil* or coping was added to the parapet, along with Greek Revival features, thereby transforming the Spanish Pueblo building into one bearing the imprint of the Territorial Revival Style. Given that the artisans of the St. Francis Cathedral installed the brick coping, it is likely that they also added other American-era features. In 1927, Margretta S. Dietrich acquired the property, joined both wings, eliminated the zaguán, and modernized the interiors. (When still partitioned by the zaguán, the deed explicitly required that the main doorway remain open for access to the dance hall and well.) A jacal or wattle-and-daub structure, consisting of cedar uprights, is situated on the northern half of the parcel. Nedra Matteucci, owner of the amazing Nedra Matteucci Galleries, and her husband, Richard, acquired the Juan José Prada House in 1989. Since then, Nedra, operating in her capacity as designer and art connoisseur, recruited designer Gene Law for the wondrous transformation of the home's interior design.

The Native arts of New Mexico and the US Southwest span a wide variety of cultural traditions, media, materials, applications, and technologies, both indigenous and introduced. While ceramics and textiles dominate the market in Southwest Indigenous and Native arts, the proliferation of both folk and traditional crafts has increased the variety of media and techniques available. From the figurative ceramics and storyteller bowls of the Cochiti Pueblo potters through to the *parfleche* or Plains Indian, Apache, and Ute war shields crafted from elk and heavy buffalo rawhide and today used as hide containers and elaborately painted boxes, Native arts have had to contend with the expanding market for commercially and mass-produced kitsch that continues to flood the market for all things construed "Indian" art. Even so, Pueblo, Diné, Apachean, Comanche, Ute, Paiute, Pawnee, and the Genízaros of Abiquiú and beyond remain purveyors of the ancestral traditions of the American Southwest, while pivoting to include innovations in technologies and techniques appropriate to expanding the repertoire of the people. Pictured on following pages are Ute and Apache quivers, beaded moccasins, Diné concha leather and silver belts, colorfully decorated Ute and Apachean *parfleche* war shields and containers, rawhide saddle bags, and Hopi *tablita* headdresses.

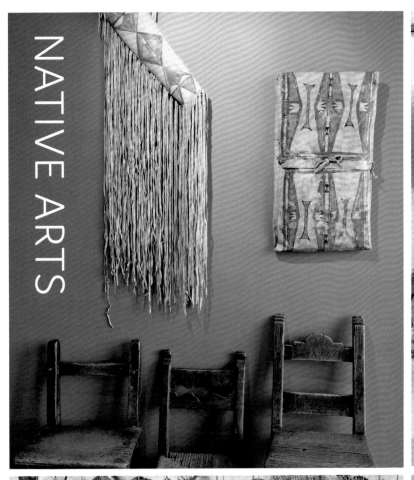

NATIVE ARTS

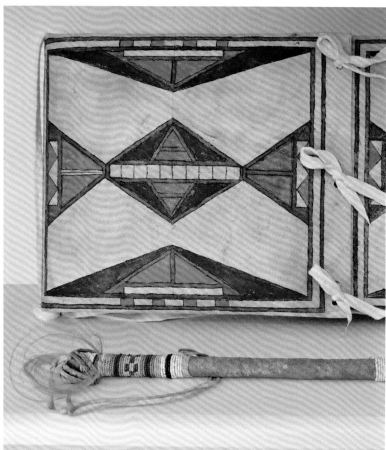

Casa Nonomaque
1985, 2009

Constructed in 1985, this splendid Spanish Pueblo and Territorial Revival Style home and guest house sit atop a hill overlooking the Sangre de Cristo Mountains to the east. The wonderfully appointed interiors feature peeled-beam vigas, Saltillo tile flooring, kiva fireplaces, exuberantly painted Spanish colonial and Mexican folk furnishings, as well as both historic and contemporary art. Casa Nonomaque is filled from floor to ceiling with masterfully crafted works by a host of famed northern New Mexican artisans. The exteriors in turn feature vintage wood plank and wrought iron gates and doorways, a brick-paved veranda with Territorial Revival white-painted colonnades, Greek Revival door and window trim boards, and wonderfully landscaped grounds replete with quaking aspens and coyote fencing. Owners Curt and Christina Nonomaque recruited designer Annie O'Carroll to oversee a complete remodel centered on paint and tile in 2009. Furniture includes antique pieces by William Penhallow Henderson and José Dolores López, as well as work by contemporary artists Luis Tapia and Sergio Tapia. Curt and Christina love being surrounded by the colorful creations of such noted Santa Fe and El Rito area artists as Patrociño Barela, Horacio Valdez, Gustave Baumann, Nicholas Herrera, and Felipe Benito Archuleta. Herrera's *Dos Amigos* (1982), crafted from the front end of a 1951 Chevy pickup truck, is a tribute to his cousin and close friend Tomás, killed in an automobile accident. The collective artistry represented in Casa Nonomaque stands as a wonderful tribute to the artisans of Santa Fe and northern New Mexico.

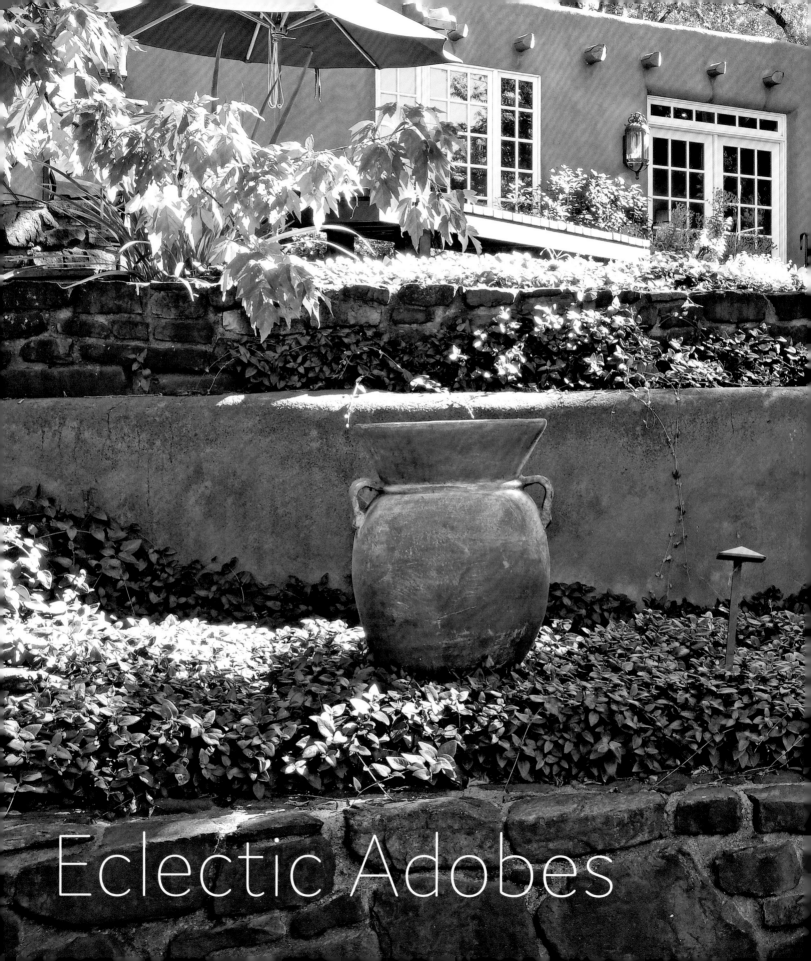

Eclectic Adobes

Casa Lucero

1817

Dated to 1817, this double-walled adobe Spanish Pueblo Style building was the home of the Lucero Family of Santa Fe. Like the parajes of the eighteenth century, Casa Lucero retains a *torreon* or defensive tower that has since been converted over to use as a wine cellar. The residence was modified in the late nineteenth century to conform to the Territorial Revival Style of the 1870s. Later occupied by Santa Fe Mayor Edward Safford from 1905 to 1915, it was long referred to as the Safford Estate. Lew Wallace, the territorial governor of the late 1870s and noted author of the historical adventure story *Ben-Hur: A Tale of the Christ*, occupied the home for a period after a fire at the Palace of the Governors, where he maintained residence as governor. Currently, the adobe is owned by David de Wetter, who came into possession of the home in 2016. De Wetter, it turns out, is a third cousin twice-removed from the early twentieth-century owner, Mayor Edward Safford. Under the ownership of David, the home underwent significant renovations from 2017 to 2018 and today is wonderfully appointed, with a mix of historic and contemporary furnishings and features. In addition, the lush gardens that envelop the adobe beautifully complement the serene and historic character of the grounds.

Casa Natalie Fitz-Gerald
1996, 2013

This Alameda Hill compound, situated off East Alameda on the historic east side of Santa Fe, dates to the late 1700s. This contemporary Spanish Pueblo Style residence was built in 1996 and was first owned by Lloyd and Janet Abrams. The house was later acquired by Charlene and Bruce Geiss before being bought by its current owner, Natalie Fitz-Gerald, the proprietor of Casa Nova, a unique home decor and gift gallery featuring the works of female South African artists. Like her gallery, Natalie's home is teeming with a spectacular array of Amerindian and African art and culture. Upon acquiring the home on Alameda Hill, Natalie quickly set about planning for the remodel in 2013. Her creativity paid dividends, as the design and ambience of the home are truly exceptional.

Casa Frank/Sugiyama
1820, 1930

Casa Frank/Sugiyama was built in 1930 as an addition to the east end of what was once a 12,000-square-foot hacienda compound dated to 1820. The hacienda originally consisted of a one-room adobe house, and over the years grew to become a four-acre estate that encompassed multiple buildings. During the late 1990s, the estate was subdivided into several condominium units. Before being partitioned, the pueblo-style home was remodeled by architect William Lumpkins in 1968. Among the renovations were those to the dining room and the conversion of the former private chapel to the main bedroom. Another example of Lumpkins's work may be found in the masterful design of the wrought iron gate leading into the garden. The house was last remodeled in 2018, at which time a sitting room was added. According to the owners, David Tausig Frank and Kazokuni Sugiyama, the home's thick adobe walls and deep-set doors and windows all combine with the height and scale of the rooms to amplify the warmth, comfort, and eclectic air of this historic building.

Casa Neumann

1924

This charming Pueblo Revival adobe, located along Bishops Lodge Road in Santa Fe, was constructed in 1924. The lush grounds are replete with quaking aspen and a flagstone walkway into the succulent and dry gardens leading to the studio. Andrew Lyons Design & Drafting and landscape designer Donna Bone of Design with Nature both worked their magic to see through the enhancement and remodel of the home, with the latest renovations completed in 2017. Originally owned by Wallie Neumann, the home's Pueblo Revival features include post-and-beam construction, hand-adzed vigas, an outdoor eating area, both raised and kiva fireplace features, and traditional and contemporary art and custom furniture.

Casa Acequia Madre

1900

The timely intervention and restoration of this Pueblo Revival Style adobe by Lucille "Lupe" Murchison of the Lupe Murchison Foundation of Dallas, Texas, was key to its preservation. Situated along the channel of the Acequia Madre proper, a nearly four-hundred-year-old Spanish colonial ditch that feeds the heart of Santa Fe, this particularly quaint and charming adobe was built in 1900. The diminutive adobe building retains much of its original hardware and features vigas in all rooms, skylights, a pewter fireplace, and both raised and kiva fireplace features. In addition to a whitewashed portal and outdoor horno, the property is circumscribed by coyote fencing. Perhaps one of this historic building's most interesting claims to fame is that American actor, playwright, author, screenwriter, and director Sam Shepard rented the home for a period in the 1980s in his initial forays toward a courtship with Academy Award-winning actress Jessica Lange.

Casa Lovato

1905, 2017

Located on Santa Fe's historic east side, Casa
Lovato was built in 1905. The adobe structure is unique in its aesthetic, exuding a mix of
old Santa Fe meets Africa, with a mid-century
twist. Currently owned by Lisa Neimeth, a noted
ceramicist, and Peter Dickstein, the home was
integrated into what was originally a part of the
Lovato family compound. The compound was
eventually partitioned into a collection of individ-
ual homes and remodeled by the current owners in the period spanning 2017 through 2000.
During the renovation, the hundred-year-old
remains of an old brewery were recovered. Among
the most distinctive features of this historic adobe
are the Catalan, thin-tile, or timbrel vaults.
Other special features include the kiva fireplaces
nestled into both the kitchen and living room
areas, the peeled-beam vigas, diminutive nichos
or niches, and the stained-glass windows that
illuminate the tiled stairway. Lisa and Peter are
also particularly fond of the tile work and wooden
cabinetry and plan to enhance both the landscape
and hardscape with a stone tub, fireplace, and
cooking areas along the portal.

Artists' Casas

Casa Jensen-Nye
1990

Casa Jensen-Nye was the first labor of love by El Guique, Ohkay Owingeh area builder Carlos Jaramillo who built the adobe for himself and his wife in 1990. A gabled adobe with peeled-beam vigas and latilla ceilings, the ranch style home is clad in stucco with mudded adobe interior walls and open partitions. A mixture of brick, flagstone, and mud floors describes the interior spaces and exterior portal. With the exception of the main bedroom, the house, measuring 1600 square feet, features a predominantly open floor plan partitioned by wonderfully fashioned pueblo-style bancos and contoured and stepped adobe half walls. The current owners, artists Lisa Jensen-Nye and Ben Nye, have remodeled the home to suit their aesthetic sensibilities and meet their day-to-day needs, and the contoured adobe walls and raw wood ceilings remain from the original construction of the house. Lisa handcrafted many of the ceramic objects that make up the decor, while Ben produced many of the photographs that grace the walls. Situated some fifty minutes north of Santa Fe, the house is nestled in the rich and fertile farmland of northern New Mexico.

COCINAS

FARMERS MARKET

Casa Padilla/Tapia

c. 1700s

As with another eighteenth-century Spanish Pueblo period adobe of the region, the Juan José Prada House of 1768, the Casa Padilla/Tapia was once subdivided by a zaguán, since enclosed. Situated astride the vestiges of El Camino Real de Tierra Adentro dated to 1598—the almost 1,600-mile Spanish royal road connecting the southern terminus of Mexico City to Okhay Owingeh Pueblo just north of Santa Fe—this historic adobe was built proximate to the fortified paraje of Rancho de las Golondrinas. Provisionally dated to the early seventeenth century, the paraje at La Ciénega was host to the legendary Spanish military leader and colonial-era governor, Juan Bautista de Anza, who cited the fortified paraje in his expeditionary report of 1780. Casa Padilla/Tapia was likely one of several such adobes that formed a hamlet that worked to support the Rancho. Today, the Casa is the home of the dynamic creative duo of acclaimed Santa Fe writer and journalist Carmella Padilla and renowned Chicano folk artist, sculptor, printmaker, and conservator Luis Tapia, whose impactful and colorful works grace the whole of the adobe. Carmella has authored a host of groundbreaking books and articles on a wide variety of topics centered on the art history and culture of northern New Mexico, including her 2008 publication titled *El Rancho de las Golondrinas: Living History in New Mexico's La Ciénega Valley*.

The folk arts of Santa Fe and northern New Mexico represent a panoply of local, regional, and traditional works representing the melding of Pueblo, Spanish, Mexican, Hispano, Asian, African, and Euroamerican borrowings and inspirations crafted for local needs, and by extension, the tourist industry. The demand for folk art is largely the product of utilitarian or practical and religious needs in localized or traditional community settings. Their creators have long been construed artisans and craftsmen and women, as opposed to fine artists. Such hand-crafted popular arts span the gamut from *ex-votos*, or painted tin or copper *retablos* and other votive offerings, wood carving, metalwork, lacquered tables and chairs, religious icons, baskets, leatherwork, and ceramic effigies. Here, the works of artists Luis Tapia, Felipe Benito Archuleta, Ron Rodriguez, Maria Romero Cash, Cordova Martinez, and Aguilar include fire screens, handcrafted furnishings, Mexican lacquered tables, carved *santos*, tin turkeys, metalcraft bikers, and the "Lowrider Nativity" of Nicholas Herrera, among others.

Billy Schenck
House and Studio
1965

World-renowned landscape architect John Brinckerhoff Jackson designed, built, and landscaped this "Plantation" Pueblo Revival Style adobe as his personal residence in 1965. Situated in an idyllic setting replete with a natural spring and rolling hills, and surrounded by ancient black poplar trees, the residence is the ideal setting for the current owners, the artist Billy Schenck and Rebecca Carter. The house doubles as Billy's studio, and is also used to display their sizable collection of Western Americana, including historic paintings and Pueblo and other Southwestern ceramics. To enhance the intimate and inviting character of the home, Billy undertook the restoration and remodel of the home in 1996 and 1998. In addition, he designed a host of light fixtures and impressive pieces of furniture that enhance the warmth and ambience of the residence. The American Indian–themed wood and metal dining room chandelier was designed by Billy and crafted by Rick Merrill of Safford, Arizona, and serves as a wonderful complement to the historic furnishings and Native American craft traditions represented.

Casa Ramona Scholder

c. 1870, 1900

The Galisteo Basin long served as a crossroads for early Puebloan peoples engaged in the trade of turquoise and malachite from the Cerrillos Hills. Twelfth-century population movements resulted in the establishment of several large Pueblos dated to the late twelfth through sixteenth centuries. In 1816, the village of Galisteo was founded and nineteen Hispanic families settled the community and built sizable walled adobe compounds. These compounds, such as that of Casa Ramona Scholder, were built, and rebuilt, many having fallen into ruin. As such, the Territorial Revival Style features of this residence date to well over 150 years and reflect mid-nineteenth-century American-era Greek Revival influence. This is particularly true of the doors and windows of the main facade, with its impressive portal. In the courtyard, reached through a wooden gateway, equally ancient cottonwood trees and a giant apricot tree stand as vestiges of that time. Originally the home of the Mora family of Galisteo, the residence was previously owned by Major and Eliza Felton and was acquired by the current owner, Ramona Scholder, in 1972. For Ramona, a favorite feature of the residence is embodied in the "graceful fireplace on the red brick patio…[which]… has seen many friends and family over the years, all enjoying the warmth and [the] beauty of a crackling fire and fragrance of piñon and cedar, another Spanish tradition."

Tom Joyce
House and Studio
1986, 1990

With formal training as a blacksmith, internationally recognized artist Tom Joyce is a master in the art and science of forging iron. Working from his studios in Santa Fe, New Mexico, and Brussels, Belgium, Tom's work spans the creative gamut from forged and cast-iron sculpture to drawings, photographs, videography, and mixed media installations. Originally built as his studio in 1986, the structure was transformed by the artist into a home three years later. Completed in 1990, the home was a labor of love in which Tom played many roles, not the least of which centered on his function as architect and landscape designer of the whole of the complex. As both owner and builder of the home, Tom was aided in its construction by family, friends, and neighbors. His facility with adobe brick making, plastering, and masonry, as well as the creation of vigas and latillas, however, was the product of his mother's mastery of building skills acquired from having studied and worked with solar pioneer Peter von Dresser. With a turquoise blue corrugated sheet-metal clad gabled roof characteristic of nineteenth-century northern New Mexican adobe homes, its breathable architecture, and natural solar heating, the house provides refuge from the summer heat, while retaining warmth and fostering relaxation during the frigid winters.

Cinco Pintores

Casa Applegate

1921, 1970, 2016

Renowned artist Frank Applegate's iconic first home, located on Camino del Monte Sol, helped define the Spanish Pueblo Revival Style of Santa Fe. To that end, the main facade features a second-story balcony that emulates those of the Spanish mission churches of the eighteenth century. Constructed in 1921, this was the first of many houses that Applegate designed and built with his friends, the legendary modernists known as Los Cinco Pintores. Their adobe homes just south of Canyon Road were known for wild parties and a bohemian lifestyle. In the 1970s, William Lumpkins, a pioneer in passive solar design, added an expansive southwest-facing room with massive vigas and a wall of windows for his client Miriam White, the founder of the Green Party of Santa Fe. David Cantor and Sydney Cooper, the current owners, have sought to maintain the historical integrity of Applegate's original vision.

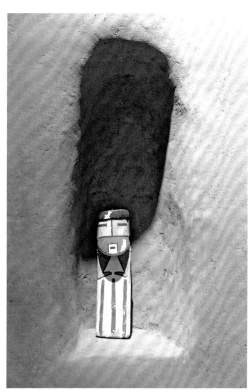

Casa Bakos-Atwood

1921, 1957

Master painter Jozef Bakos was a founding member of the art collective Los Cinco Pintores, since deemed instrumental in launching the modern art movement in Santa Fe. The group's five painters, also known as the "five nuts in five mud huts," built their homes in a row on Camino del Monte Sol, the heart of Santa Fe's budding art colony of the 1920s through the 1930s. The artists themselves designed and built two of the four adjoining houses, along with substantially remodeling existing buildings. Casa Bakos-Atwood was hand-built by Bakos, who was a carpenter as well as an artist, in 1921. According to current owner Lynda Atwood, all of the homes of Los Cinco Pintores "survive as a strong and tangible expression of the artists' aesthetic, work practices, and craftsmanship." And the adobes "express the lives and personalities of their creators probably more than any other artists' properties remaining in Santa Fe from the period." Since that time, the home has undergone several rounds of remodels and renovations. In 1957, Bakos enclosed the courtyard with an adobe wall. From 1988 through 1990 the kitchen was remodeled by Lee Deidrich and the main bedroom and studio by Louis Briones. Lynda facilitated several renovations, working to enhance the hardscaping of the courtyard and adding skylights to the home.

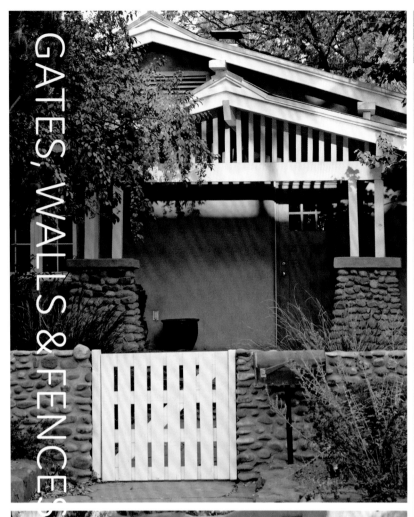

GATES, WALLS & FENCES

Casa Shuster

1923

All five members of Los Cinco Pintores, Will Shuster, Wladyslaw "Walter" Mruk, Willard Nash, Fremont Ellis, and Jozef Bakos, were beholden to the famed artist and preservationist Frank Applegate for their respective homes. Having advanced each member of the group credit toward the purchase of their respective parcels, Applegate assisted each artist with the design and construction of their adobe homes. With little to no experience with adobe construction, Shuster recalls "What a bunch of ham builders we were!" Even so, after the artist completed his adobe, the Shuster family lived in the home for more than fifty years. The residence was designed and built in the Pueblo Revival Style, which was a requirement of all homes built upon those lands offered by the original landowner, Frank Applegate himself. The house subsequently underwent renovations and remodels, in 1988 and 1999, respectively. Its interiors feature post-and-beam construction with adzed beam ceilings, historic wrought iron Spanish colonial and Mexican hardware, nichos, and masterfully carved Solomonic columns astride the staircase and railings. Today, proud owners Laurie Larsen and Tom Stoner seek to maintain the integrity and charm of this historic home, while at the same time preserving its historic origins.

DOORS

Ranches

Windland House
1997

Windland House, formerly known as the Fisher Landau Residence and Community Center, is situated on the 3,250-acre Saddleback Ranch, nestled between two rural New Mexican villages, Galisteo and Lamy. Suby Bowden and John Morrow of Morrow Bowden Architects, with Joe D'Urso of Joe D'Urso Design, designed and built the award-winning 6,103-square-foot Windland House in 1997. The original owner, Emily Fisher Landau, collaborated closely with the architects who, in their own words, sought "design solutions with bold references to American plains architecture…designed to differentiate between the domesticated and the wild landscape." As such, shaded pathways and windbreaks permit gentle transitions between buildings on the property. Architect Suby Bowden notes that "selections of elegant materials and finishes, combined with pure architectural forms in a minimalist vocabulary…[were intended to]…create sanctuary spaces" in this contemporary architectural setting. Significantly, the Saddleback Ranch properties were designed to exhibit a major museum-quality private art collection within an over 31,000- square-foot building area. The architects were awarded top State Honors from the AIA (American Institute of Architects) in 2003, and subsequently, the Jeff Harnar Award for Contemporary Architecture in New Mexico.

Morning Star Ranch
2008

Featuring the integration of traditional Southwestern pumice and adobe construction with an admixture of both Spanish Pueblo and Territorial Revival Style features, this technology-enhanced 9,000-square-foot living space in Cerillos, New Mexico, was constructed relatively recently. The design and build were the collaboration of designer Jody Keut and architect Miguel da Silva of da Silva Architecture. Completed in 2008, the estate consists of a sprawling high desert hacienda and private observatory featuring the latest state-of-the-art photovoltaic, hydronic, and astronomical technologies available. According to da Silva, the complex was transformed over the course of a three-year period "from a modest and remote 1,200-square-foot observatory torreon into a palatial observatory and hacienda facility, integrating the torreon, and additionally featuring a conference room and custom spa facilities." The unmistakable integration of Territorial Revival Style elements is conjoined with a Spanish Pueblo bell wall, Greek Revival window and door piercings, zaguánes, Pueblo-styled rooftop ladders, post-and-beam construction, shepherd's bed, and a rooftop cacti garden within the context of a conventional courtyard scheme and fortress-like mein.

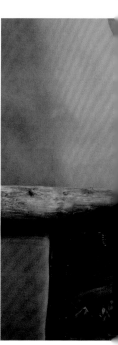

WEAVING

The fiber arts of the American Southwest and Four Corners area developed from a particularly ancient tradition of crafting with animal hair, plant fibers, and eventually basketry. Where the Ancestral Pueblo are concerned, loom-crafted textiles first appeared among the Hohokam of the Sonoran Desert of Arizona and northern Mexico by AD 1000, and at Chaco Canyon, New Mexico, by AD 1100. The wood and fiber looms that revolutionized the craft of weaving took three primary forms in the Southwest, and these included those of the vertical or upright loom or narrow-waist looms of Chaco Canyon in the period spanning AD 1100 through 1300. Thereafter, such looms caught on among the Pueblos of the Rio Grande and north and central New Mexico, and the Four Corners. The third type was that of the horizontal looms of the Tohono O'odham (Papago) and Akimel O'odham (Pima).

The arrival of the Spanish brought with it the introduction of white and brown wool fibers shorn from Churro sheep. The ready availability of introduced wool and treadle looms, and the Spanish imposition of tribute in blankets, readily displaced cotton that was once dominant among the Ancestral Pueblo and Diné or Navajo weavers. Today, both history and tradition compete with an increasingly voracious market for handcrafted Pueblo, Diné, and Hispano blankets, rugs, and tapestries.

Contemporary Casas

Casa Sierra Vista
2004

Designed and built by architect Mark DuBois and landscaped by Paula Hayes over the course of a three-year construction timeline spanning 2001 through 2004, this majestic contemporary Santa Fe home has been host to many significant guests, as well as to museum and political fundraisers in recent years. To create a rapport between art, architecture, and the land, this minimalist building stands in contrast to the naturalistic setting that envelops its frame. Replete with panoramic glass windows, cast-concrete walls and finishes, steel cladding, and wooden piers and floors, the breathtaking vistas are such that the home's interiors appear to extend into the surrounding landscape filled with white and blue spruce and Scotch and Monterey pine. The ultimate effect is that of calm, with casual surroundings and relaxed interior furnishings lending to the air of tranquility that the house evokes. The cohesive aesthetic is palpable to all who enjoy and visit this mountain redoubt.

John and Tanya Young House
1992, 2000, 2005

When celebrated architect John Young and his wife, Tanya, originally purchased this awe-inspiring contemporary Santa Fe home in 1992, it was an altogether unimpressive building. Despite that fact, the new owners spied its potential, particularly the magnificent views to be had of the Galisteo Basin and surrounding mountain ranges. In 2000, John launched a wholesale renovation of the residence, with the goal of blurring the line between nature and structure. To accommodate a new and larger open floorplan, an extension was added, enhancing the living, dining, and kitchen areas. Amendments included the installation of a cantilevered waxed-concrete bar and stainless steel kitchen, with a bleached-oak sliding door to partition off the bedroom and bathroom. John describes the residence in terms of its "earth-colored cantilevered concrete portal [that] wraps around three sides of the house enclosing a courtyard of local volcanic rock. Shafts of sunlight penetrate gaps in the long west wall, built to shelter the courtyard from the prevailing wind." Two large ventilation flues were installed to moderate internal temperature without the need for air-conditioning. These were designed to draw fresh air into the home by way of convection, thereby maintaining comfort throughout the year. Sizable sandstone slabs were laid over a subfloor for the installation of a radiant heating system. By the end of the remodel, completed in 2005, the external adobe walls and pine vigas were all that remained of the original building.

Charles Moore House
2007

Internationally renowned Mexican architect Ricardo Legorreta designed this colorful contemporary Santa Fe townhome in 2007. The exteriors of the townhouse development evoke Puebloan-like buildings by way of the massing of cubic structures with a decidedly geometric character. With its exterior stucco walls painted in earthy reds, oranges, bright yellows, purples, and pinks, however, the interiors paled by comparison. The exuberant colors of the exterior elevations inspired the homeowners, Charles "Chuck" Moore and family, to stay true to that formula for the interiors of the home as well. Legorreta's delightful interplay of light, shadow, and volume generated an internal dynamism for the display of contemporary paintings of varying sizes and shapes. To expand upon Legorreta's vision, Chuck worked to ensure that the grounds were an equally calming space for relaxation. As such, the Moores launched their landscaping plans with the planting of some thirty-five aspen and twenty-two piñon pines to shade the sun from the west, and these have since become large-shaded container gardens with a fifteenth-century Native American gate serving as the partition between two large exterior living spaces. According to Chuck, "Our gardens have become so much a part of our living space due to the incredible Santa Fe climate, the golden sunshine, and bright cerulean blue skies that we can enjoy for six months of the year."

William Miller House

2004

Built in 2004, the William Miller House stands as an outstanding example of contemporary New Mexican architecture. The architect, Stephen Bucchieri, sought to integrate a minimalist design such that volumetric space, and strategically oriented elevations and glazing, highlight the majestic views enjoyed by the site. The owner, William Miller, sought to maximize that modicum of solar geometry, light, and shadow, such that accommodating his extensive art collection would prove a central design concept in the planning of the home. In fact, William construes his abode as an art gallery. The home is bisected over the principal axis and central corridor with a linear skylight oriented on true north. This feature produces a dynamic light array that spans the entirety of the home and its main hall and art gallery during the course of the day. The interior spaces are complemented by the unfettered views of the horizon with its truly spectacular hilltop views of two mountain ranges and the distant Colorado border. Among other salient moments, the home hosted a political fundraiser with Michelle Obama on behalf of her husband, at that time the future president of the United States.

Beverley Spears House

2014

Owner and architect Beverley Spears designed this wonderfully evocative and well-appointed contemporary home overlooking the city of Santa Fe. Drawing on her expertise with both traditional New Mexican architecture and the early monastic churches of Mexico, the house features barrel vaults or bovedas, and thick adobe-like walls in a passive solar setting. Beverley designed the home in a contemporary New Mexico style while paying homage to houses built on a more traditional design plan. Examples of this can be seen represented in the insulated thick concrete exterior walls, flat roofs with a roof deck, and a lengthy portal replete with a white-walled entrance. The house was intended as a sanctuary for the owners, Beverley Spears and Philip Crump, and one exuding calmness and serenity. The barrel vaults were constructed to elicit the character of the cloisters and early monastic churches of Mexico, while also providing tranquil interior spaces. The theme of the sanctuary is continued throughout the house, with a Zen garden, roof deck, fountain, and natural native landscape. Beverley and Philip especially enjoy the concrete water-trough and stainless steel scupper fountain, situated just outside the living room glazing, which provides a reflecting pool that projects sunlight onto the ceiling vault of clear pine boards inside.

Patricia Stanley House
1994

Designer Barbara Horowitz of BHS Design of New York teamed with renowned New Mexico architect John Midyette to see through the design and build of this extraordinary contemporary Santa Fe residence. With an original build in 1994 and a remodel by the current owner, Patricia Stanley, in 2017, the home deploys the refined use of handsome materials and a sophisticated color palette dominated by whitewashed walls and teak wood, acid-washed concrete floors, pine beams, and rafters. The overall effect evokes an elegant simplicity and a wondrous sense of serenity overlooking the "City Different" below. Having recruited the original architect and designer for the remodel, Patricia upgraded the home with a modern kitchen and three up-to-date bathrooms. The home provides the ideal space within which to showcase African, Amerindian, and contemporary works of art and collections of objects from around the world. Patricia's favorite feature is the panoramic window offering majestic 270-degree views of the Sangre de Cristo and Sandia Mountains by day, and the lights of the city of Santa Fe by night.

BIBLIOGRAPHY

Berke, Arnold. *Mary Colter: Architect of the Southwest*. New York: Princeton Architectural Press, 2002.

Booker, Margaret Moore. *The Santa Fe House: Historic Residences, Enchanting Adobes, and Romantic Revivals*. New York: Rizzoli, 2009.

Booker, Margaret Moore. *Southwest Art Defined: An Illustrated Guide*. Tucson: Rio Nuevo Publishers, 2013.

Bunting, Bainbridge. *Early Architecture in New Mexico*. Albuquerque: University of New Mexico Press, 1976.

Cross, Mark H. *Encyclopedia of Santa Fe and Northern New Mexico*. Santa Fe: Caminito Publishing, LLC, 2012.

Gellner, Arrol. *Red Tile Style: America's Spanish Revival Architecture*. New York: Viking Studio, 2002.

Griffith, Jim. *Saints of the Southwest*. Tucson: Rio Nuevo Publishers, 2000.

Hammond, George P., and Agapito Rey. *The Rediscovery of New Mexico, 1580-1594*. Albuquerque: University of New Mexico Press, 1966.

Harris, Richard. *National Trust Guide: Santa Fe. America's Guide for Architecture and History Travelers*. New York: John Wiley & Sons, Inc., 1997.

Jeffery, R. Brooks. "From Azulejos to Zaguanes: The Islamic Legacy in the Built Environment of Hispano-America." *Journal of the Southwest*, 45(2003), 289-327.

LeBlanc, Sydney. *Secret Gardens of Santa Fe*. New York: Rizzoli, 1997.

Mather, Christine, and Sharon Woods. *Santa Fe Style*. Design by Paul Hardy. Photography by Robert Reck, Jack Parsons, and others. New York: Rizzoli, 1986.

Mendoza, Rubén G. "Adobe," in *Encyclopedia Latina: History, Culture, and Society in the United States*, Volume 1, pp. 16-17. Ilan Stavans, Editor in Chief; Harold Augenbraum, Associate Editor. Danbury, Connecticut: Grolier Academic Reference, an imprint of Scholastic Library Publishing, Inc., 2005.

Mendoza, Rubén G. "Hispanic Sacred Geometry and the Architecture of the Divine," in *Journal of the Southwest* 48(4): iii-xiv. Winter, 2006.

Mendoza, Rubén G., and Melba Levick. *The California Missions*. Text by Rubén G. Mendoza. Photography by Melba Levick. New York: Rizzoli, 2018.

Mendoza, Rubén G., and Melba Levick. *The Spanish Style House: From Enchanted Andalusia to the California Dream*. Text by Rubén G. Mendoza. Photography by Melba Levick. New York: Rizzoli, 2021.

Mendoza, Rubén G., and Jennifer A. Lucido. "Of Earth, Fire, and Faith: Architectural Practice in the Fernandino Missions of Alta California, 1769-1821," in *Colonial Latin American Historical Review*. Spring, 2014, pp. 1-47. Albuquerque: University of New Mexico, 2014.

Noble, David Grant. *Pueblos, Villages, Forts & Trails: A Guide to New Mexico's Past*. Albuquerque: University of New Mexico Press, 1994.

Padilla, Carmella (ed.). *Borderless: The Art of Luis Tapia*. Long Beach, CA: Museum of Latin American Art, 2017.

Padilla, Carmella (ed.). *Conexiones: Connections in Spanish Colonial Art*. Santa Fe: Museum of Spanish Colonial Art, 2002.

Padilla, Carmella. *El Rancho de las Golondrinas: Living History in New Mexico's La Ciénega Valley*. Photography by Jack Parsons. Santa Fe: Museum of New Mexico Press, 2009.

Schuetz-Miller, Mardith. *Architectural Practice in Mexico City. A Manual for Journeyman Architects of the Eighteenth Century*. Tucson: University of Arizona Press, 1987.

Spears, Beverley. *American Adobes: Rural Houses of Northern New Mexico*. Albuquerque: University of New Mexico Press, 1986.

Usner, Don J. *Sabino's Map: Life in Chimayó's Old Plaza*. Santa Fe: Museum of New Mexico Press, 1995.

Weber, David J. *On the Edge of Empire: The Taos Hacienda of Los Martinez*. With Anthony Richardson. Albuquerque: University of New Mexico Press, 1996.

Weigle, Marta (ed.). *Hispanic Arts and Ethnohistory in the Southwest*. Santa Fe: Ancient City Press, 1983.

Whiffen, Marcus, and Carla Breeze. *Pueblo Deco: The Art Deco Architecture of the Southwest*. Albuquerque: University of New Mexico Press, 1984.

Wilson, Chris. *The Myth of Santa Fe: Creating a Modern Regional Tradition*. Albuquerque: University of New Mexico Press, 1997.

Wilson, Chris, and Oliver Horn. *The Roque Lobato House: Santa Fe, New Mexico*. Photography by Robert Reck. Santa Fe: Schenck Southwest Publishing, 2014.

GLOSSARY

Compiled by Victoria Gagnon
After Mark H. Cross (2012), Richard Harris (1997), and Marta Weigle (1983)

acequia [*uh*-sey-kyuh; *Spanish* ah-se-kyah] An irrigation ditch generally identified with northern New Mexican agriculture. The *parciantes*, which draw water from the ditch, are organized into an acequia association headed by a *mayordomo*, or ditch boss.

Acequia Madre [*uh*-sey-kyuh; *Spanish* ah-se-kyah], [mah-drey; *Spanish* mah-*th*re] The "mother ditch" or main trunk of a local canal system for irrigation.

adobe [*uh*-doh-bee] A sun-dried brick made of adobe clay, sand, and straw; and, accordingly, a building constructed from such adobes. The basic building block for the original Santa Fe Style.

alacena [ah-lah-seh-nah] A recessed cupboard built into an interior adobe wall, often featuring decorative wooden doors.

Anasazi [ah-n*uh*-sah-zee] Ancestral Pueblo, identified with such sites as Chaco Canyon and Mesa Verde. Coined by the Diné or Navajo to identify Ancestral Pueblo.

Ancestral Pueblo [an-ses-tru*h*l] [pweb-loh; *Spanish* pwe-blow] See Anasazi.

araña [ah-rah-nyah] "Spider" or multi-armed "chandelier" in wood, wrought iron, or tin.

banco [bang-koh, bahng-] A bench generally built into an interior adobe wall.

boveda [boh-veh-dah; *Spanish* boh-beh-dah]: (Sp. *techo curvo, cúpula*), masonry vault, dome, cupola.

bulto [bul-to; *Spanish* bool-toh] Carved, three-dimensional *santo*, or depiction of a saint.

caliche [k*uh*-lee-chee] A calcium carbonate layer on or just beneath the surface of the soil. Used for producing durable floors and coating walls.

calle [kah-yeh] "Street" or other formal pathway through a town or village.

campo santo [kam-poh, kahm-] [san-toh, sahn-; *Spanish* sahn-taw] "Holy ground," a cemetery consecrated by the bishop or other high church official.

canales [ka-nal; *Spanish* kah-nahl] Rain spouts that extend through the parapets of Santa Fe Style buildings to channel rainwater off the roof and away from the walls.

capilla [kah-pee-yah] "Chapel" or other place of worship, whether within a church precinct or family compound.

casita [kuh-see-tuh; *Spanish* kah-see-tah] "Little house," usually a guest house on a larger property occupied by caretakers or guests.

Catalan vault Timbrel or thin-tile vault, or bóveda, originally introduced by the Romans.

descanso [dehs-kahn-soh] "Resting place." Originally a place where pallbearers rested en route to the graveyard. Also, a roadside shrine to accident victims.

El Camino Real de Tierra Adentro [kah-mee-noh], [rreh-ahl], [tyeh-rrah], [ah-dehn-troh] The 1,591-mile-long Spanish royal *camino* or King's road that spanned the distance between Mexico City and San Juan Pueblo, New Mexico, in the period from 1598 to 1882. One of four extending into the northern Frontier.

El Morro [(Balearic, Valencian) IPA: / mo.ro/…"morro"] Notable promontory and mesa-top thirteenth-century pueblo located on the old Zuni-Acoma Trail of west central New Mexico. Identified by the sixteenth-century Spanish as El Morro, or "the Headland," and by the Zuni, as *A'ts'ina*, or "Place of writings on the rock," for its accumulation of some eight hundred years of Pueblo, Spanish, and early Anglo American rock art inscriptions.

farolito [far-uh-lee-toh, fahr-] "Little lantern," a Christmas decoration consisting of a brown-paper bag weighted with sand, and lit from within by a candle.

faux adobe Faux, or fake, adobe; a term used to describe a lath and plaster or other building designed to appear as though it were an adobe.

hacienda [hah-see-en-duh; *Spanish* ah-syen-dah] House, outbuildings, and land owned by a hacendado or wealthy person, such as a large landholding or an in-town estate.

hogan [hoh-gawn, -guhn] Diné or Navajo structure of the Four Corners region, traditionally octagonal in shape, with a smoke hole in the center of the roof and doors facing east to catch the light of the morning sun.

kachina [kuh-chee-nuh; *Hopi*: ka'tsʲina] A carved and costumed figure or doll representing Pueblo deities, created by the Hopi and Zuni to teach children about their ancestors and supernatural guardians.

kiva [kee-vuh] Pueblo ceremonial space, generally circular in plan, and at least partially or wholly subterranean. Also known as *fogónes* or corner fireplaces.

kiva fireplace [kee-vuh] [fahyuhr-pleys] Barrel or beehive-shaped corner fireplace in many a Santa Fe Style adobe.

Kokopelli [kōkə'peli] Humpbacked flute player depicted in rock art, thought to be a water conjurer.

latillas [luh-tee-uh; Spanish lah-tee-yah] A wooden ceiling consisting of intertwined small poles or slats spanning beams or vigas.

luminaria [loo-m*uh*-nair-ee-*uh*; *Spanish* loo-mee-nah-ryah] Term for a bonfire or a lantern, depending on the region. In Santa Fe, *luminaria* refers to a bonfire. In Albuquerque and the rest of the country, the word refers to the candle-in-a-bag lantern that Santa Feans identify as a *farolito*.

Mexican Period The period spanning 1821 and 1848, when the Mexican Republic controlled what is now the American Southwest, ending with the Treaty of Guadalupe Hidalgo.

milagro [mee-lah-groh] "Miracle," also, a pot metal trinket designed to be pinned to the robes of a Catholic saint in a church or shrine. Molded in the shape of a body part to indicate to the healing saint the location of the supplicant's distress.

miraculous staircase Staircase used to access the choir loft in the Loretto Chapel of Santa Fe. Unique in design, craftsmanship, and materials, and built by a mysterious craftsman in 1878.

Mission Revival Architectural style characterized by silhouetted shapes that mimic the old missions, with large flat stucco surfaces, often punctuated by deep windows and doorways.

morada [moh-rah-dah] Penitente chapel, a small, usually windowless adobe building that serves as a meeting place for the secretive Hermanos Penitentes, or "Brotherhood of Penitents."

Mudéjar [moo-*the*-hahr] (adj., ES *relativo a musulmanes*), a subject Muslim of the Christian reconquest of the Iberian Peninsula; Iberian Gothic and Islamic architectural style of the twelfth to fifteenth centuries.

nicho [nee-choh] A niche, or small cut-out in an adobe wall, used to display a *bulto* or saint, or other religious or secular work of art.

parroquia [pah-rroh-kyah] Parish church.

petroglyph [pe-tr*uh*-glif] A pecked rock geometric, anthropomorphic, or zoomorphic engraving or inscription of the type found just west of Santa Fe, or in the Mesa Prieta Petroglyph park.

pictograph [pik-t*uh*-graf, -grahf] A painted rock art element rendered in red or yellow ochre, charcoal, or other mineral pigments.

plaza A central courtyard or town square. Spanish Royal regulations mandated that towns and villages be organized around plazas.

portal A long, narrow porch. On a Spanish Pueblo Style building, the portal roof is supported by rough-hewn posts.

Pueblo Revival Inexact name for Spanish Pueblo Style architecture, which combines Spanish building techniques and Pueblo forms. A misnomer that ignores the Spanish contribution.

reja [rah-j*uh*] Split juniper or cedar branches (also called *cedros*) layered above vigas in Spanish Pueblo style ceiling construction.

repisa [re-pi-sa] Shelf or mantlepiece.

reredos [reer-dos, reer-i-, rair-i-] Painted or carved screens displayed behind a church or Mission altar.

retablo [rreh-tah-bloh] A Catholic folk art devotional painting on wood or tin, often depicting a saint. Or the main altar screen of a church or chapel.

sala [sah-l*uh*] Room, usually the living room. Sala can also reference a central hall in an adobe.

Saltillo tile [sahl-tee-yaw; *Spanish* sahl-tee-yoh] Naturally earthen-colored square or rectangular, reddish-brown fired floor tiles that originated in Saltillo, Mexico.

Santa Fe Style A uniquely distinct and hybrid architectural style that celebrates the fusion of local cultures and traditions, spanning those of the Pueblos, Spanish colonial, Mexican, and Anglo American territorial eras.

Santa Fe Trail Wagon route from Independence, Missouri, to Santa Fe that served as New Mexico's second major source of trade between 1821 and 1880, after which the Santa Fe Railway displaced the utility of the trail.

santero [sahn-ter-oh, san-] An artist, such as the master craftsman Luis Tapia of Santa Fe, who carves and paints *santos*, or produces depictions of saints in various media.

santo [san-toh, sahn-; *Spanish* sahn-taw] A carved and/or painted depiction of a saint.

santuario [sahn-twah-ryoh] Sanctuary. The Santuario de Chimayo is renowned for its "holy dirt," which draws the faithful from throughout the US Southwest and beyond.

shepherd's bed A raised sleeping platform of wood and adobe, or bed, placed directly over or adjacent to the kiva fireplace to take advantage of the rising heat.

sipapu [si-pa-pu] (*nan-sipu*, "belly-root," or "heart of the earth"). In the Pueblo creation myth, the hole through which the first people emerged from the underworld. Kivas each feature a hole in the floor representing the *sipapu*.

Spanish Colonial Period The three-hundred-year period (1521-1821) during which the Spanish controlled significant portions of the Americas, including the American Southwest and Southeast, Central America, and Western South America.

Spanish Pueblo Style One of two distinct types of Santa Fe Style architecture, representing the architecture of the Spanish colonial period, before kiln-fired bricks and milled window and door frames were widely available.

Spanish Revival A hybrid style of adobe and masonry architecture blending Andalusian, Spanish colonial, and indigenous traditions.

straw appliqué The art and craft of decorating crosses and other items with gold-colored straw or corn husks.

Talavera [tah-lah-vair-*uh*, tal-*uh*-] Colorful Mexican tile of Mudéjar or Moorish design used in backsplashes, tiled pavements, door jambs, or fountains, and patterned after that originally produced in Talavera de la Reina, Spain.

Territorial Period The period spanning 1848 through 1912, when New Mexico was a territory of the United States prior to its admission to the Union.

Territorial Revival Style One of several distinct architectural variations on the Santa Fe Style, with Victorian- or Greek Revival-styled enhancements, including the addition of kiln-fired bricks or coping used to trim the top of parapet walls.

torreon [tawr-re-awn] A defensive tower with gun ports commonly deployed at the *parajes* or roadside inns along El Camino Real during the Spanish colonial period.

trastero [trahs-teh-roh] A tall, hand-carved Spanish colonial cabinet or cupboard for dishes.

Turquoise Trail A circa fifty-four-mile National Scenic Byway along Highway 14 in northern New Mexico linking Albuquerque and Santa Fe. Corresponds to a string of ancient turquoise mines and ghost towns.

viga [vee-*guh*] Wooden roofing beams, typically peeled ponderosa pine, at times carved and painted.

zaguán [sah-gwahn](*Arabic ustawaan*, "porch, breezeway") Open space hidden from the public eye.

zapato [*zuh*-pah-t*oh*; *Spanish* sah-pah-toh] Carved and corbelled wooden brackets.

Zozobra [soh-soh-brah] Spanish for "worry." With origins in the El Pasatiempo arts festival launched in 1926, and intended as a parody of the Fiesta de Santa Fe, Zozobra, a fifty-foot-tall effigy or marionette of Old Man Gloom, is burned annually at the Fort Marcy complex. Introduced to the cycle of festivities by Will Shuster.

ACKNOWLEDGMENTS

We gratefully acknowledge the many institutions, architects, designers, homeowners, representatives, staff, and friends who gave their time and attention to accommodating our many editorial requests, inquiries, and site visits. Each of them is heir to this exploration of the grand architectural traditions of the Pueblo people and the Spanish Style in the Americas. This book would not have come to fruition without the vision and commitment of our publisher, Rizzoli International Publications, and especially publisher Charles Miers and our editor, Douglas Curran. We are forever grateful to the Rizzoli team, and in particular to Douglas for his keen aesthetic eye, unflagging leadership, and promotion of this labor of love, as well as to David Skolkin, for his sensitive and elegant design. We are grateful for the introductions and immeasurable assistance provided by Antonio Chavarria, curator of ethnology, Museum of Indian Arts & Culture / Laboratory of Anthropology; Elysia Poon, IARC director, School of Advanced Research; Suby Bowden, architect, Bowden and Associates; and Beverley Spears, architect, Spears Horn Architects. Mendoza was afforded invaluable editorial and technical support and assistance by Jennifer A. Lucido, lecturer, Archaeology Program, CSU Monterey Bay; Gaylord R. McCurdy, photo technical support; and John Thomas "J. T." Taylor for his invaluable editorial, written, and research contributions in the preparation of the house descriptions. Victoria Gagnon of the CSU Monterey Bay Archaeology Program in turn prepared the glossary in her capacity as research assistant and transcriptionist to Archives & Archaeology. Melba Levick wishes to thank Matt Walla and John Vokoun for their technical assistance.

We further express our heartfelt gratitude to the many homeowners and newfound friends who opened their doors and welcomed us to Santa Fe and beyond. They include Karl and Susan Horn, Christopher Watson, Donna and Hal Hankinson, Wayne and Linda Palla, Joe and Bunny Colvin, Tom Applequist and Charles Newman, Temple and Mickey Ashmore, Lauren Hunt, Matthew and Penny Rembe at Los Poblanos, Ramona Scholder, Tom Joyce, David Cantor, and Sydney Cooper, Lynda Atwood, Laurie Larsen, Peter Dickstein, and Lisa Neimeth, Tanya and John Young, Jeanne and Michael Klein, Charles Moore, William A. Miller, Philip Crump and Beverley Spears, Patricia Stanley, Andrea Fisher, Suby Bowden, Nedra Matteucci, Curt and Christina Nonomaque, David de Wetter and Michael Namingha, Natalie Fitz-Gerald, David Frank, and Kazokuni Sugiyama, Madeleine Gehrig, Ray Landy and John Grey, Malcolm Lazin, Lisa Jensen-Nye, Carmella Padilla and Luis Tapia, Billy Schenck and Rebecca Carter, Barbara Mauldin, Dee Ann McIntyre, Susan Stella, Eleonor Brenner, Louisa Stude Sarofim, Douglas Atwill, Jon Bosshard, David Margolis and Jeanne Moss, and Leticia Quinn.

Among those who graciously opened their galleries, shops, cultural centers, and businesses to us in our exploration of the Santa Fe Style, we acknowledge Andrea Fisher Gallery; Nedra Matteucci, Nedra Matteucci Galleries; Chimayo Weavers; Allissa Mitti; Nicolas Flechin Museum, Taos; Jordan Young, Executive Director, Women's International Study Center; Natalie Fitz-Gerald, Casa Nova Gallery; Ira and Sylvia Seret, Inn of Five Graces; Katherine Wells, Mesa Prieta Petroglyph Project / Wells Petroglyph Preserve; Laban Wingert, Architect; Elysia Poon, SARS; Aaron Gardener, Minge House; Shiprock Santa Fe Gallery; Morning Star Gallery; Justin Mayrant, Tin maker; Sheri Brautigan; Elizabeth Kay; Rachel Preston Prince; Ivan and Allison Barnett, Patina Gallery; and Jodi Apple.

Finally, the authors acknowledge their respective families. To that end, Rubén Mendoza is so very grateful for the loving support of his wife, Linda Marie, and the infinite patience and understanding of his daughters, Natalie Mendoza-Schlegel and Maya Mendoza Taylor. Melba Levick in turn wishes to acknowledge and thank her devoted husband, Hugh Levick, without whose patience, assistance, and support this book would not have been possible.

First published in the United States of America in 2023 by
RIZZOLI INTERNATIONAL PUBLICATIONS, INC.
300 Park Avenue South, New York, NY 10010
www.rizzoliusa.com

Publisher: Charles Miers
Editor: Douglas Curran
Production Manager: Barbara Sadick
Managing Editor: Lynn Scrabis
Copy Editor: Victoria Brown
Proofreader: Sarah Stump

Designed by David Skolkin Design, Santa Fe, NM

Printed and bound in China

2023 2024 2025 2026 2027 / 10 9 8 7 6 5 4 3 2 1

ISBN-13: 978-0-8478-9914-2
Library of Congress Control Number: 2022944437

Visit us online:
Facebook.com/RizzoliNewYork
Twitter: @Rizzoli_Books
Instagram.com/RizzoliBooks
Pinterest.com/RizzoliBooks
Youtube.com/user/RizzoliNY
Issuu.com/Rizzoli